IN
LOVE
WITH
EARTH

IN
LOVE
WITH
EARTH

Testimonies and Heartsongs
from an Environmental Elder

Marc McGinnes

Community
Environmental
Council

Published in the United States of America by

Community Environmental Council
26 West Anapamu Street, 2nd Floor
Santa Barbara, CA 93101
www.cecsb.org

an imprint of

Mercury Press
INTERNATIONAL
Mercury Press International
www.mercurypress.com

Publisher's Cataloging-in-Publication Data

Names: McGinnes, Marc, author.
Title: In love with earth : testimonies and heartsongs from an environmental elder / Marc McGinnes.
Description: Santa Barbara, CA : Community Environmental Council/Mercury Press, 2018.
Identifiers: ISBN 978-0-9990342-1-7 (paperback) | ISBN 978-0-9990342-9-3 (ebook)
Subjects: LCSH: Environmentalists--United States--Biography. | Earth Day--History.| Oil spills--California--Santa Barbara Channel. | Environmental protection--United States--History. | Environmental sciences. | Environmental law. | BISAC: BIOGRAPHY & AUTOBIOGRAPHY / Environmentalists & Naturalists. | SCIENCE / Environmental Science. | LAW / Environmental. | HISTORY / United States / State & Local / West (AK, CA, CO, HI, ID, MT, NV, UT, WY)
Classification: LCC GE56.M337 A3 2018 (print) | LCC GE56.M337 (ebook) | DDC 333.72092--dc23.

Cover and back cover photographs: NASA
Cover Design and author photo: Isaac Hernández
Interior Design: Quike Hernández

For all of the Earthangels who are here now
and for all those who are coming
and will keep on coming after I am gone.

*"In gratitude is the exaltation
of the human spirit.
Through greed
all that is given is lost."*

— Marc McGinnes

Table of Contents

"History will judge you.
And as the years pass, you will
ultimately judge yourself on the extent
to which you have used your gifts to lighten and
enrich the lives of your fellow man.
In your hands is the future of your world and
fulfillment of the best qualities
of your own spirit."

— Senator Robert Kennedy

Foreword

It's a powerful thing to love the Earth. While the world is filled with opportunities to marvel at its full, jaw-dropping glory, we rarely do.

Instead, most of us barrel through lives that are both technologically over-connected and emotionally under-connected. We fill the in-between spaces with Twittery bursts of information and occasional videos of cute animals. Admittedly, the monkey who has adopted a kitten is amazing, but rarely do we allow ourselves to sense the full magnitude of the natural world. Rarely do we get what an incredible, blue marble we live on, calibrated perfectly for life.

For Marc McGinnes, one such awe-inspiring moment came when he saw an image taken from the moon on Christmas Eve, 1968—the Earth rising in the distance. This Earthrise photo has since become culturally symbolic to the point of archetypal. But for Marc, standing in a darkened lecture hall seeing it for the first time, it was love.

With the spirit of an improv artist—whose only rules are to say "yes" to what has been invited and then add to that invitation—in that moment, Marc began to embrace the role of Whole Earth Citizen. In *In Love With Earth*—part memoir, part love letter, part call-to-action—he takes us on his journey to explore what that citizenship means, including the individual environmental rights and responsibilities that come with it. Along the way he sails us through the high ideals and sweeping successes of the dawning modern environmental movement, as well as through dips of delusion and despair.

It's a timely reflection, with the 50th anniversary of one of the catalysts of the environmental movement: a massive oil spill off the shores of Santa Barbara, California on January 28, 1969. As the largest oil spill in US waters at that time (later to be surpassed by the 1989 Exxon Valdez spill in Alaska and then again by the 2010 Deepwater Horizon spill in the Gulf of Mexico), the Santa Barbara spill became one of the most visible environmental crises of that era. Marc—early in his legal career and wrestling with a desire to align his life around his values—quickly moved his wife and newborn son to Santa Barbara.

His timing couldn't have been better, as the field of environmental law was just emerging. In the several years following—thanks in part to the moral outrage and political will that emerged from the oil spill—critical legislation and institutions that we still rely on today were put into place, including the Environmental Protection Agency, National Environmental Policy Act, Clean Water Act, California Coastal Commission, and California Environmental Quality Act.

Locally, the spill led to the formation of Get Oil Out!, the Environmental Defense Center, the Environmental Studies program at the University of California at Santa Barbara, and the organization that I would later take the helm of: the

Community Environmental Council (CEC). Marc was at the center of each of these pioneering institutions, serving as a founding Board member of CEC and involved in the protection of places that are central to Santa Barbara's identity: East Beach, Hammonds Meadow, More Mesa, and the Gaviota Coast.

I was born into this world just a short time before the events that sparked the formation of this new movement which changed the course of Marc's life. Following on the heels of the Baby Boomers, my generation now comprises his "just-in-time" Earthangels, who are currently tackling the complex challenges of climate change, rampant consumerism, the dismantling of environmental protections, and systemic injustices.

Like many who have dedicated their lives to environmental activism, in *In Love With Earth*, Marc, at times, is literally and figuratively at sea. But even in despair he remains an open learner and embraces synchronicity—those "meaningful coincidences," as Carl Jung called them. Learning to follow the subtle drop of breadcrumbs to discern your life's journey is a skill that requires quieting the brain's chatter to hear the softer tugs of intuition. Marc has found that some synchronicities have a luminous quality to them, drawing you along like clues to a mystery. You must answer that ringing phone. Follow that car. Read that book.

One such moment occurred in my office in November 2015. Marc and I were talking over tea, about the struggle with maintaining hope. For environmental activists, this is a common theme, as we deal daily with existential threats. On this day we discussed how atmospheric carbon dioxide levels had rocketed beyond anything humans have experienced in four million years, with scientists increasingly warning of our entrance into the "sixth mass extinction" event in nearly half a billion years.

Marc wondered aloud if hope is even necessary, and I saw his point. There is a kind of hope that takes the shape of magical thinking, that feels saccharine or shallow, like something off a Hallmark card.

But once again, the timing was perfect, as I had on my coffee table my latest read: *Active Hope* by Joanna Macy and Chris Johnstone. In the book they explore a more mature kind of hope grounded in gratitude—the kind that helps us envision what we want and triggers a desire to work against difficult odds, even the potential for failure.

This book became the next breadcrumb on Marc's path, and he soon returned to UCSB after a long hiatus in teaching to offer a class on "Hope That Works." As I later shared with that class, to me this means finding the space beyond denial of what's happening, and beyond blind optimism that someone else will fix the problems. It means owning the realization that no one is coming to save us, and that we must execute our own rescue. It means tapping into a fierce love for life.

Through this lens, it's possible to approach our future more creatively, and avoid the sense that a dystopian ending is a *fait accompli*. And that's critical now, as we navigate our way through cycles of extreme weather with increased frequency—including excessive heat, extended drought, year-round fire seasons, coastal storms, more intense precipitation such as microbursts and "rain bombs," and ensuing flash floods and debris flows.

It is also critical as we imagine the rebirth of the modern environmental movement: one that brings in those who were not at the table 50 years ago, including low-income people, women, the elderly, youth, immigrants, and people of color. In other words, the next chapter must engage those who have been disproportionately burdened by social injustices and who have fewer resources to respond to the negative impacts of climate change and other environmental threats.

For all of this we will need courage, gratitude, and a willingness to truly love the blue marble that is our home. Now more than ever we need the voices of our elders. We need their learnings, their commitment, their experience and their wisdom.

Sigrid Wright
CEO/Executive Director,
Community Environmental Council

Sigrid Wright is the first woman CEO/Executive Director of Community Environmental Council, a nearly-50-year environmental nonprofit based on the California Central Coast. She was raised in Eugene, Oregon, started her environmental career in Washington, DC and has been leading place-based environmental activism for more than 20 years. She also serves on the Santa Barbara County Commission for Women.

Atomic City Kid

1

The world's first full-scale nuclear reactor went "critical" and began producing plutonium about 35 miles from the house in Richland, Washington where I lived with my single mother, Fern, and older brother, Drue, in 1945. The reactor was located on the top-secret Hanford site of the Manhattan Project, situated along the banks of a remote stretch of the Columbia River. Razor wire topped the perimeter fencing, and deadly-force security measures were in effect.

We had lived there since 1943, when I was two and my name was James Marc Lazenby. The house had been assigned to my mother because

Newly constructed Richland, circa 1943, one of the "Secret Cities" of the Manhattan Project, where author Marc McGinnes was raised.
Photo courtesy of US National Archives.

1951 white prefab house, typical of the Secret Cities, including Richland, WA, providing workforce housing for the Manhattan Project. *Photo courtesy of US National Archives, Department of Energy, Hanford History Project, Washington State University, Tri-Cities.*

she was a member of the Hanford workforce. It was a prefabricated plywood structure nailed together in the shape of a box. The whole place shook and rattled in the massive dust storms that blew across the sagebrush-covered flatlands.

We and most of mother's large family had moved to Richland from Salt Lake City where they had fallen on hard times during the Great Depression. Other Mormon relatives had been part of the earlier exodus out of Utah to find work further up the Columbia on the Grand Coulee Dam.

The first batch of Hanford plutonium was carried in the backseat of a sedan, down the road along the Columbia River to Portland, Oregon, next to be delivered by rail to the Trinity test site in New Mexico.

There some of it was detonated in the world's first test of a nuclear weapon (codename "The Gadget"), and a few weeks after that, some more of it was flown across the Pacific to Tinian Island, where it was fitted into the atomic bomb (codename "Fat Man") that was dropped by an American bomber over the city of Nagasaki, Japan on August 9, 1945.

"Fat Man" type nuclear weapon, circa 1945, as detonated over Nagasaki, Japan in World War II. The bomb is 60 inches in diameter and 128 inches long. It was the second nuclear weapon ever to be detonated. It weighed about 10,000 pounds and had a yield equivalent to approximately 20,000 tons of high explosive. *Photo courtesy of Los Alamos Scientific Laboratory, Harry S. Truman Library & Museum.*

That single bomb killed an estimated 70,000 people. It also blew the top off the secrecy that had surrounded what was going on at Hanford. The frontpage headlines of the Richland Villager newspaper shouted, "PEACE! Our Bomb Clinched It! Japs Surrender! Plant Will Not Close!"

I remember my mother laughing and crying as she showed the newspaper to Drue and me, and how it felt to watch and listen to her and Drue as they took turns reading the words out loud.

That night as we lay in our bunk-bed talking softly with the lights out, six-year-old Drue explained to four-year-old me that Richland was now famous for winning the war and that our mother and everyone else in the family would get to keep living here and not have to move somewhere else.

In the years immediately after the end of WWII, additional nuclear reactors were constructed and brought online at Hanford, bringing more workers to Richland and also providing a significant economic boost to the neighboring cities of Kennewick and Pasco, 10 miles downriver on opposite banks of the Columbia between its confluence with the Yakima

Atomic cloud rises over Nagasaki, Japan, August 9, 1945. *Photo by Lieutenant Charles Levy, US National Archives.*

and the Snake rivers. These three cities were known as the Tri-Cities. The plutonium-production operations at Hanford soon became the area's dominant industry.

Richland was dubbed "The Atomic City" by its fledgling Chamber of Commerce, who then organized the first of the community's annual Atomic Frontier Days parades and celebrations in 1947. These events included military bands

Richland's The Villager, August 14, 1945.
Courtesy of Marc McGinnes Archives.

with troops and weapons, along with floats and convertibles with dignitaries, queens and princesses, and we kids bringing up the rear on our bikes festooned with crepe paper, with playing cards clothes-pinned to the fender struts to make rat-a-tat-tat sounds like the machine guns of the fighter planes we saw in the war movies we watched for hours on a ticket that cost 11 cents.

Richland High School "Bombers" logo, 2018.

The mascot of Richland's high school was changed from the Columbia High School Beavers to the Richland Bombers, and the logo became (and still is) an atomic mushroom cloud blast. The football coach there became well-known for exhorting his players to visualize what the mascot of the opposing team (a Pasco Bulldog? a Kennewick Lion?) would look like when hit by the blast wall from an atomic bomb.

Dipnet fishing at the Cul-De-Sac of Celilo Falls, Columbia River, Oregon, ca. 1957.
Photo by US Army Corps of Engineers [Public domain], via Wikimedia Commons.

The same year that the high school was renamed, so was I. Our mother told Drue and me that our last names were now McGinnes. She showed me my new name on what she said was a new birth certificate, which I thought looked funny compared to my previous one. I asked if my real name was still Marc, and when she said yes, I felt better about it all.

I and every kid I knew who was good at football couldn't wait to get on the Richland Bombers and to get to wear our letterman's jackets around town, and on Friday nights get to blast the other team to bits.

I was nuts about baseball and football, hooky-bobbing on the back bumper of cars slowly traversing snowy streets, snow-ball fighting, water-skiing, running along behind the mosquito-control fogging Jeeps in clouds of sweet-smelling DDT in the summertime, horseback riding out near "the Indian burial grounds," playing knock-on-doors-and-run, going on watermelon raids, sleeping out in the cemetery, building forts and bunkers of all kinds, and going on car rides with my grandfather down along the Columbia to watch Native American fishermen spear and net salmon as they attempted to leap upriver over the rapids and waterfalls on the Indian reservation near The Dalles, Oregon.

My mother and stepfather, both office workers, were nuts about buying more and newer stuff with which to "keep up with the Joneses" in a race to get in on (and not get left out of) the blessings of post-war prosperity. Subjected to massive and unceasing advertising propaganda onslaughts, they were prodded into believing that it was their civic duty to become avid, even rabid, "consumers".

Like it or not (my grandparents and a couple of uncles hated it), "Buy New Stuff!" seemed to be becoming a new national chant, if not a motto. America was to become a cornucopia overflowing with stuff that could and had to be gobbled up and discarded to make room for more stuff coming through.

In this way, as I later came to understand, the capitalist regimes of the United States and its allies saw their best hope of winning over the hearts and minds of their people in order to successfully meet the challenges posed by the increasingly formidable communist regimes of the Soviet Union and China and their allies during the Cold War years.

The communists fought the capitalists (those who strive to govern us today as they did then) to a standstill in Korea, and the communists decisively won the race to be first to launch an orbiting satellite into space. We heard rumors that the Soviet Union had its own atomic cities where they made hydrogen bombs that were more powerful and deadly than ours. Whether or not you had gulped down or had gagged upon the "strength through shopping" propaganda devised in order to sustain capitalism, such news was deeply unsettling to the bowels.

My stepfather and a neighbor got all caught up in the "let's all buy bomb shelters" craze before their wives finally shot down the plan. "If everybody else gets blown up, I don't want to be around to see who crawls out of holes to carry on," was how my mother put it when she let my stepfather know he would have to choose between the bombshelter and continuing to live with us.

One moonless night, I watched in stupefaction and awe as the blinking light of Sputnik 1 moved (how?!) across the whole, bare, star-freckled belly of the sky. I had forgotten to breathe, and it seemed as if I had

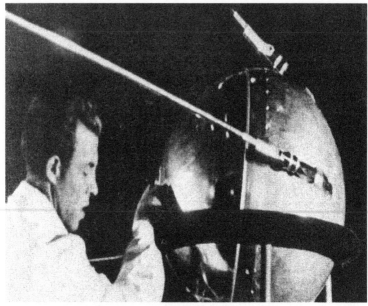

On Oct. 4, 1957, Sputnik 1 successfully launched and entered Earth's orbit. Thus, began the space age. The successful launch shocked the world, giving the former Soviet Union the distinction of putting the first human-made object into space. This historic image shows a technician putting the finishing touches on Sputnik 1, humanity's first artificial satellite. *Photo by Asif A. Siddiqi /NASA.*

gone deaf. I felt both uplifted and opened wider than the surfaces of my body. I stayed outside, transfixed, until it came and went again a couple of hours later.

As I watched it come and go for the third time that night, I felt older, something like a young man. I was 16, and I had in my head the idea of becoming the Ambassador of the United States to the Soviet Union. Either that or the next Mickey Mantle or part of the crew on the first mission to land on the moon. In the last case, I wondered if that crew would make the first landing or would come in second to the Soviet cosmonauts.

I had no access to any of the top brass who ran the Richland/Hanford military outpost with whom to talk about what was going on and what they were thinking about. The smartest people in Richland who were accessible to me were the teachers at the schools I attended, and from a handful of them

I received encouragement to ask questions, think for myself and make the choices that have brought me to the place I am today.

One of them was a stern woman whose English class taught me the importance of humility and gratitude as means of keeping my feelings of pride and self-importance in check. Another was a chemistry teacher from whom I learned no chemistry at all but whose insights about American history, politics, and economic thinking prepared me to think critically and unconventionally about such topics at Stanford, in law school, and as a citizen of my communities thereafter.

Another was a history teacher and athletic coach who was gay, and whose courage and compassion I have tried to emulate throughout my life.

Without such teachers, I don't know how I could have put up with life at home under the reactionary dictatorship of my stepfather and the on-again-off-again gyrations of my mother's relationship with me.

From him: "The trouble with you, Marc, is [fill in the blank]."

From her: "Either you do as I say, Marc, or I'm going to tell your father about [fill in the blank]." In my mother's case, the first of those words didn't have to be spoken, but were silently conveyed by an expression of her face that meant to me, "I am prepared to let your father really lower the boom on you!"

From both: "If that is the way you're going to be, then you must or must not [fill in the blank]." They were not to be reasoned with or appealed to in passing judgment.

From me: words of appeasement that burned in my mouth and resentments that embittered my feelings toward both of them to the breaking point.

Looking back, I regret that I could not have done more to be a better son to them both and a better brother to my siblings. Learning forgiveness for myself and of others has been a lifelong pursuit.

During my childhood years, one particular person stood taller in my eyes than anyone else, even though he was less than three years older: my brother Drue. In the beginning was the word, and the word was Drue, and from the unwritten Book of Drue I got my most trustworthy clues of what was going on about anything worth knowing about. I would have been lost without him.

Author James Marc Lazenby, at age three. *Photo courtesy of Marc McGinnes Archives.*

When Drue was five (and I was not quite three), he took off from home one day with me in tow to have a look around the wider world. When I got tired, he hailed a bus to pick us up, and we rode for what seemed like a very long time as passengers got on and off. Finally the driver said, "Okay, boys, we're here!"

He dropped us off at the police station, where they had cocoa. Just as Drue was about to ask for a second round, our mother showed up.

"Hi Mommy! Are you lost too?" Drue said. There was a picture and story about it in the newspaper, and it was fun to hear my mother's version of it.

I had a passing relationship with organized religion when my mother, an apostate or "jack" Mormon, persuaded me to become a member of that church's lower priesthood (Aaronic). I think she figured that her lapses would be overlooked if I took to the doctrine and became a "good" Mormon. It was like being the second son in an Italian family who was given to the church to become a Catholic priest as a means of getting in good with the Bishop and the other guys in high hats and elegant pumps.

My priesthood duties consisted of:

1. Breaking slices of Wonder Bread into bite-size pieces of the body of Christ and passing them out on a silver tray to members of the congregation,
2. Filling small paper cups with tap water (the blood of Christ) and passing those out,
3. Giving occasional "two-and-a-half-minute talks" of an uplifting nature from the podium in front of the congregation, and

4. Going around with an adult higher-level priest (named Melchizedek) making house calls on people during dinner hours for the purpose of letting them know that the church had its eye on them and was disappointed in their poor attendance (we had the numbers to prove it).

In this manner, I was able to:

1. Cadge as much Wonder Bread on Sunday mornings as I could get away with, wadding it into dense balls that I pocketed and stealthily savored later during the services,
2. Quench my thirst even on fast-days,
3. Learn valuable public speaking skills, and
4. Come to despise what seemed to me like strong-arm tactics practiced by the church to keep its followers (sourcing tithes of 10% of income) in line.

The two-and-a-half-minute talks were perfect preparation for keeping my presentations as an environmental lawyer and advocate within the strict time limit imposed by courts and governmental bodies.

My idea of God during my church-going days wasn't pretty. God seemed like a vengeful, unwelcoming, all-seeing presence. He could and did watch everything I was up to and he was usually angry about what he saw. As a result, I sought only the most limited, utilitarian contact with the divine.

When I was about eleven, on days when my baseball team had a game, I would put on my uniform, go into the chapel, take off my cap—still wearing my cleats, my glove beside me—and pray to hit a home run. It was an all-American scene worthy of Norman Rockwell. I prayed for success in baseball, and it worked, not because any higher entity cared about my puny game, but because I became a master of visualization.

As I prayed, I pictured myself going through all the necessary motions, with just the right timing. The first time I prayed like this, I hit two home runs. God was on my side! That kept me going until I fell into a slump, striking out with the bases loaded in an important game. After that, I felt betrayed by God, and I stopped going to church.

By then, I was also old enough to refuse my mother's wishes, insisting that I wouldn't attend church as a proxy for her anymore.

As a young baseball player, I learned not only how to move from visualization to realization in order to perform at my best (what I called "seeing into being," even then); I also learned how to promote myself as a rising star, someone to keep an eye on. Someone to root for.

I made an arrangement with the sports editor of the local newspaper to relay the scores and highlights of games in which I played via telephone, and since I was a good player, my name showed up regularly on the sports page. Years later, this same man shared with me that he was positive I would make it to the top of the baseball world as a sports agent, if not as a player.

My favorite baseball coach often said to me, "Marc, you have the tools to become a great ballplayer. What you have to do is to look and act like one."

Portraying one of my favorite Major League players, I stepped to the plate with a fat wad of Tootsie Roll in my cheek, just like the wad of chewing tobacco my hero had. I fouled off the first pitch, stepped back from the plate and spit a stream of dark juice onto the ground, just as my hero did.

"Time out!" the plate umpire roared. "Young man, clean that up right now or I'm tossing you out of the game!" It stung when he muttered, "Who are you supposed to be, anyway?"

Marc's High School senior portrait, class of 1959. *Photo courtesy of Marc McGinnes Archives.*

I heard laughter from people in the stands. Ouch! I chewed and swallowed the candy. The pitcher made a mistake on his next pitch, and the ball came waist-high down the middle, and I hit it far over the fence in left-center.

As compensation for being mostly unhappy at home, I sought to be regarded with respect and, yes, admiration from my classmates, teachers, coaches and others in the community. I was the captain of the sports teams I played on and an elected leader of the student organizations to which I belonged. In my senior year at Kennewick High School I was president of the student body, co-captain of the football team, chief editor of the school newspaper, the lead in the senior class play, and was voted Mr. Senior (Most Likely to Succeed) by my classmates.

At my high school, I was among several other athletically talented students, some of whom went on to play professionally. I was deeply competitive, and in my environment, winning was really everything. We fought together on the field, and sometimes we fought against each other in the school parking lot to keep our place in the pecking order. I didn't win all my fistfights, but I never called it quits.

Once a guy hit me with brass knuckles and nearly knocked my head off. I got up and kicked his ass to a month of Sundays. Fifty years later, we laughed about it at our 50th class reunion. We joked about going outside to let him see if he could settle the score after so many years.

The sour relationship between my stepfather and me prompted my desire to be as little financially reliant on him as possible. From the time I was in the tenth grade, I worked at all kinds of jobs: sorting mail at

Marc as a junior quarterback and senior co-captain for the Kennewick Lions. *Photo courtesy of Marc McGinnes Archives.*

the post office, waiting tables and washing dishes in restaurants, selling encyclopedias and vacuum cleaners door-to-door, cleaning boats in the marina, loading and unloading trucks and railroad cars in the lumber yards, working at Sears as a sales clerk and delivery man, diving into water traps at the golf course to retrieve and sell golf balls, baby-sitting, umpiring Little League baseball games, setting pins at the bowling alley, anything to make a buck.

When I was in high school, I worked for the city parks department, starting at four in the morning, driving a tractor to set out long aluminum sprinkler tubes on the lawns, moving them at intervals and loading them all up when my shift ended at 12:30 mid-day. I also cleaned the men's and women's bathrooms and spread fertilizer on the lawns of the city's largest park. This involved going down to the sewage treatment plant and pitchforking dried processed sewage, called sludge, into a machine called a shit-grinder.

One day a co-worker and I were pitching sludge into the shit-grinder, and it was a particularly windy day along the river where we were working. I was wearing gloves and a bandana over the lower half of my face, shielding my nose and mouth from the dust and small fragments of dried sewage.

My buddy either had no bandana or had left it in his pocket. We were talking and laughing as we worked. I had saved a good joke to pop on him, and I turned to see him roar with laughter. What I beheld and will never forget was literally a shit-eating grin, his gums and teeth outlined with the dust and grit from our labors.

Life lesson: Grinding shit in windy weather is no laughing matter.

I applied to a number of universities, including Dartmouth back East, Indiana of the Big Ten, and Stanford, over in sunny California. Although my applications were based on my ability to imagine myself on a particular school's football team or baseball team, I was lured most strongly by the prospect of getting away to the magical land of California. As kids in the middle of nowhere, we kept sharp eyes out for those golden license plates on the cars driving through town, and we always paid attention to how visitors from that dreamy land dressed and behaved. In the end, Stanford offered me a partial athletic scholarship. California, here I come!

I started out with freshman football but I immediately learned that two taller, very good quarterbacks had been recruited ahead of me, and that I would have to switch to a halfback position that mostly involved blocking and brawling rather than tossing tight spirals to sprinting receivers for touchdowns. It was definitely a step down.

I pinned my hopes for stardom on baseball instead, and I became the starting third-baseman and was elected team captain. Unfortunately, because of a wrist fracture I sustained playing football in my senior year in high school, I discovered I could no longer pop the ball like I used to. I went up to bat and was repeatedly horrified when pitches I should have driven out of the park turned into weak grounders, fly-outs and pop-ups. It was a great disappointment to realize I wasn't going to be Stanford's shining baseball star.

Luckily, I did well in my classes and was selected to join an honors section in the introductory Western Civilization course. There I met Alexander Kerensky, one of many pivotal players at that stage of my life, and he and other faculty luminaries recognized something in me and generously helped to shape my character and my future.

Kerensky had been a moderate socialist minister in the Russian Provisional Government formed after the revolution, and he had barely escaped with his life when Lenin and the Bolshevik faction came to power.

Pete McCloskey, US Congressman and 1972 presidential candidate.
Photo via Wikicommons.

He was fascinated by my stories of what life was like in Richland at the beginning of the atomic age.

I had the opportunity to discuss history with those who had been involved in the making of it, who had influenced its course with their wits and will. I was so energized in my studies in the presence of such people that, although I had never considered myself an exceptional scholar, I found myself excelling in nearly all of my classes with the glaring exception of chemistry, where I failed to attain even a gentleman's C.

Professor Paul Ehrlich was my academic advisor during my freshman year, his first year at Stanford. Later on I met Pete McCloskey, who at that time had just founded the law firm that advised the people and companies who were bringing the Silicon Valley into being. He became my mentor and advisor during my law school years and immediately thereafter.

I qualified for Stanford's Directed Reading Program, a curriculum of independent study for highly motivated students. With a diplomatic career still in mind, I wrote a proposal to study modern European history, which was critiqued and modified by a professor who informed me that I'd have to read about twice as much as I'd planned. Undeterred, I carried out the course of study, supplementing the history I was learning with courses in economics and political science.

I further widened my horizons by studying abroad, traveling to France in my junior year to attend the Stanford campus in Tours, affiliated with the University of Poitiers. I socialized with French students and people in the community who were interested in meeting American students, but it wasn't an immersion experience. We didn't always grasp the cultural significance of what was happening around us.

1936 Citroën Traction Avant 11 B. *Photo by Thomas Forsman via Wikimedia Commons.*

With one of my American classmates, I bought a 1936 black Citroën sedan which turned out to be the kind of car used by the Gestapo and the Vichy militia, the Milice, whose work it was to round up and murder Jews and members of the French Resistance. I did not know this and failed to consider why the vehicle was offered at such an exceptionally low price. Why look a gift horse in the mouth?

When we drove it around town, the car drew baleful stares and muttered remarks that were plainly unfriendly. When the situation was explained to us, we rarely drove it in France and used it instead for trips to and through other countries. In hindsight, it would have been better if had we not driven it at all.

I recently saw the same model on the street in Santa Barbara, and met its owner who obliged me by listening to my story about mine. Even though I love the car I drive now—the only Volvo faux "Woody" in the world, as far as I know—I would be tempted to trade it for the old Citroën we called Sapphire.

I vividly remember my pilgrimage to Thermopylae, Greece, an adventure of those Stanford-in-France days. There, on a bright winter day, I experienced an intense vision of the battle which took place there thousands of years before between hordes of Persian invaders against a much smaller band of mostly Spartan defenders, of whom I was one. With my comrades, I rushed to meet our enemy, slashing with my blade and shield, when suddenly I felt the searing pain of a spear-thrust into my side, and I stumbled and fell and felt myself die. Some part of "me" that

Marc's *El Volvo* "Woody". *Photo courtesy of Marc McGinnes Archives.*

is part of who I am "now" watched, from high above, the fight continue and "end."

Was this craziness or something else? It was something else. At other times and places over the years, I've had similar experiences. Imagination or something else? Something else. What is "real" in my experience is not always what I can understand, or for which there is a reasonable explanation. There is far more going on around us, I think, than we usually register.

During summers at home for my first two years at Stanford, I worked in a warehouse on the Hanford Project site, close to the nuclear reactors. On my way to work, I passed through a perimeter marked by tall fences and topped with razor wire. I had to stop at a military checkpoint to display my pass. My job was quite physical. I loaded hardware and materials onto trucks for delivery to the reactor sites.

Later in life, a connection from this humble job in the boondocks helped me nab a top-notch position at a major law firm. Also later, I was notified that I was eligible to be tested periodically to determine if my exposure to radiation while working on the site was having ill effects on my health. So far, so good, even though I glow in the dark.

As I closed out my time at Stanford, it was my intention to join the US Army. I wanted to go to the Defense Language Institute Foreign Language Center in Monterey, California to learn to speak Russian. I had this naïve notion that the way to become an ambassador to the Soviet Union or anywhere else was to join the State Department diplomatic corps and work your way up the ladder based on your skill and experience. My plan was to learn to speak Russian as a first step along that path.

Joining the Army was, I thought, the best way to learn Russian. After that I intended to enroll in the Fletcher School of Law and Diplomacy and then to begin my climb in the diplomatic corps.

Many of my fraternity brothers were in the Reserve Officer Training Corps (ROTC), and they were slated for service in the Army or Marine Corps after graduation. For them, military service was the required first step in their lives after Stanford. They financed their college careers in some part by committing to serve in the military after graduation. I had paid my way with various scholarships, student loans, and earnings from various part-time jobs. They had to go; I didn't. Most of my brothers who served in Vietnam paid a heavy price. One of them was among the first Americans to be killed there.

One of our professors was the famous civil rights and anti-war fire-brand Allard Lowenstein. When he learned of my plan to join the Army, he collared me after class, putting his hands on my cheeks as he mouthed the words, "Baby, please don't go!"

He said it so slowly and with such a look on his face that it froze me to the spot. He implored me to find something else to do for at least a year and then to reassess the situation. I followed his advice and applied as a late applicant to law school at UC Berkeley.

I am pretty sure that it was the letter of recommendation that Pete McCloskey wrote for me that prompted the admissions folks to give me the nod. His recommendation at a pivotal moment in life a few years later led me to come to Santa Barbara to pursue life-changing opportunities.

Pete was a lawyer and a decorated Marine hero who was openly against American military involvement in Vietnam. In 1967 he became a Republican Congressman, and in 1972 he ran against Nixon in the presidential primary, on an anti-Vietnam War platform.

He was widely known to be a man of steadfast principles who was willing to work with members of the opposing party to approach and resolve thorny problems in a bipartisan manner.

For that reason, Pete, a Republican, was the person that Democratic Senator Gaylord Nelson asked to join him as co-chairman of the group that planned and carried out the first Earth Day observances around the country. Earth Day was inspired in large part by the Santa Barbara oil spill and the subsequent conference on the Santa Barbara Declaration of Environmental Rights, in which I had a role. But I digress.

Pete's wise counsel and patience with me during my years in law school and first years of law practice were essential to my sticking with my legal education, and to eventually finding my niche as a public interest environmental lawyer.

Following my first semester at law school, I was astonished to find myself somewhere near the bottom of my class academically. Pete

Mario Savio on top of a car during the Free Speech Movement protests, 1964.
Photo courtesy of UC Berkeley, Bancroft Library.

refused to let me sulk, letting me know that he'd had a similar comeuppance, and telling me that some of the best lawyers he knew were in the same league with us as law students. I told myself that I was not really that interested in studying law anyway, or even becoming a lawyer. I reminded myself that I was just taking a year off to see how the situation in Vietnam unfolded.

While at law school, I took on the part-time job as the assistant sales manager at the Cabana Hotel, a mob-backed, Las Vegas-style hotel in Palo Alto. It was a surreal, glamorous atmosphere where sophistication and sleaze mingled easily. The Beatles stayed there when they came to the Bay Area, as did many mobsters when they congregated for periodic meetings on the West Coast. My job was to make cold calls to the offices of nearby businesses and distribute cards which entitled the bearer to free drinks at our bar.

For the first time in my life I met women who showed far more interest in my body than in my mind. I took it all in stride and decided to stay in law school rather than to become their toy.

In 1964, Berkeley exploded right in front of my eyes. I was with a group of friends standing outside the law school when we heard muffled shouts and chants, down the hill toward Sather Gate. We saw a guy with a big shock of hair standing on top of a car, shouting through a bullhorn to cries of "Shut it down!"

The man was Mario Savio, a powerful speaker and one of the leaders of the Free Speech Movement. He spoke to the large crowd with ease and eloquence, addressing the importance of students contesting the university's policies that banned political activity on campus. It was a critical moment, marking the rise of political and countercultural consciousness among college students across the United States. Everyone was turned on, and I was riveted. Someone lit up a doobie, and when it came around I took a hit and we all walked down the hill, as I skipped the taxation course that was as big a mystery to me as chemistry had been.

Up until then I had not been an activist; but the times were a-changing, and I decided to jump right into the fray. I helped to organize a graduate school group to support the Free Speech Movement cause, and

I joined a group of law students advising student draft-resisters who were refusing to participate in the Vietnam War.

As I began to look deeper, I realized that my country had fallen under the domination of those who had gulped down the "Domino Theory" Kool-Aid served up by the Dulles brothers and their allies, and had come to believe that if Vietnam did not remain firmly locked into the orbit of the capitalist powers, its loss would set off a chain-reaction of challenges by communists to the United State's imperial hegemony over Third World nations in Southeast Asia and elsewhere. The Domino Theory was potent, and blindly intoxicated most of its adherents.

The history of post-WWII events in Vietnam showed that its leader, Ho Chi Minh, had sought the assistance of the United States in resisting the restoration of French colonial rule. Because these efforts had been rebuffed, Vietnam had fought for its independent sovereignty and had defeated the French despite the strong backing of the United States. Rather than recognizing Vietnamese independence, the United States immediately set about plotting its overthrow.

The Domino Theory was a propaganda ploy to make American citizens believe that the defeat of Vietnamese independence was vital for the national security of the United States. It was a lie, and so the Vietnam War came to have two frontlines, one over there and another over here.

Fighting against injustice and for freedom became a driving force for me. For me, that means active resistance against assaults on one's personhood, on one's liberties, one's choices of what to believe, and on one's choices of how to live. I care deeply about people not being sub-jugated. I am committed to doing my utmost to confront injustice, not merely as an abstract principle, but in service to actual circumstances on a case-by-case basis.

Between my second and third years of law school, I had a summer clerkship at the prestigious law firm of Thelen, Marrin, Johnson & Bridges in San Francisco. My academic record was unimpressive, but to my amazement I had just the right connections to score this opportunity. As it happened, one of the firm's partners who interviewed me had a con-nection with the head of the construction company that ran the Hanford site that had hired me to work in the warehouse there. My blue-collar job

Marc McGinnes, young lawyer, around 1967. *Photo courtesy of Marc McGinnes.*

opened the door to this white-collar echelon among the legal titans of the West Coast.

Three other clerks were hired by the firm at the same time, another guy from Berkeley and two guys from top law schools elsewhere. My Berkeley classmate ranked near the top of our class. I ranked somewhere near the bottom. You wouldn't have bet on me being hired at the end of our clerkship, but I responded with gusto to a new competitive opportunity. I took the cases seriously and I produced work that impressed several of the firm's partners. At the end of the clerkship, I was offered a job as an associate lawyer upon my graduation.

In 1965, during my third year in law school, I fell in love with Kathy Snow, a young woman who later became my wife. We were introduced by her cousin, a member of the Kappa Kappa Gamma sorority where I worked as a pot boy. Kathy was a graduate student in education, and it was love, on my part, at first sight.

She told me she thought I looked like the young Paul Newman. That was a good entry. And I impressed her greatly one evening when I spelled out her first and last names in a single stream of pee on the pavement in front of the sorority house under a full moon. That seemed to seal the deal.

In 1966, when we both graduated, we planned to spend most of a year living and traveling in Europe. I talked my new law firm into deferring the beginning of my work with them and financed our trip with a fellowship from the International Rotary Club Foundation for post-doctoral study at the University of Nancy, in the Lorraine region of eastern France.

This required me to speak to chapters around the entire country, but I was soon relieved of this, when every Rotary Club within a hundred-mile radius learned how bad my French actually was. Since I hadn't impressed

Marc McGinnes on fellowship with Rotary International Foundation, 1966.
Photo courtesy of the Marc McGinnes Archives.

anyone with my skill as a speaker, I was free to pursue my own interests with Kathy and do some post-graduate research.

We set up house in a comfortable garden apartment at the rear of a hotel near the center of Nancy, France, and took the train to the

Volkswagen factory in Wulfsburg, Germany. There we took delivery of a brand new station wagon, in which we tooled all around France and several countries in Eastern and Western Europe.

Our travel bible was *Europe on Five Dollars a Day,* and by sticking to it most of the time, we were able to splurge occasionally on, say, a four-course meal and a bottle of wine by candlelight on a terrace with someone playing a violin. Once I ate a meal in the finest hotel in Sofia, Bulgaria, consisting of potatoes prepared and garnished in eight different ways. The dessert was ice cream made from, you guessed it, sweet potatoes.

We drove into Greece at the Bulgarian border and down from Thessaloniki along the coast past Mt. Olympus, to Thermopylae, where I showed Kathy the place where I had that past-life experience of having been killed in battle there. If she thought I was crazy, she didn't say so. In Athens we ran into her brother, drank a lot of retsina, and put the car on the ferry headed for Italy.

Once we drove down to Spain, took the ferry over to Tangiers, and smoked a lot of oregano that we had been told was the "very best marijuana" by the man who sold it to us. A friend of ours who was there on a break from his studies in Sweden bought a whole bunch of the stuff from the same guy, tried to smuggle it back to Stockholm where it would have made him a small fortune at that time, got caught and arrested, and then—just after calling home to report that he had ruined his life—was kicked out of the jailhouse and laughed at for having paid way, way too much for oregano.

On and off, I dabbled in legal research concerning the new European common market, but I didn't let that interfere with our pleasant bohemian, proto-hippie lifestyle. When the fellowship ran out, we returned to the States, got married in 1967, and settled down to our new life in a rented cottage in the Berkeley hills. I purchased a three-piece button-down suit, sharpened my pencils, and went to work for corporate America.

Answering the Call

2

At the Thelen law firm in San Francisco, with my own secretary and stack of casefiles to work on, everything appeared to be lined up for my personal success in the legal profession. The firm had origins beginning with Herbert Hoover, who was a friend of Max Thelen, Sr., a fellow member of the country's power elite at the highest level. At the time I worked there, the firm represented some of the most powerful corporations in the world, including Bechtel, Kaiser Industries, Standard Oil, Arabian-American Oil Company (ARAMCO) and an array of real estate developers and homebuilders.

In terms of prestige, I was unbelievably lucky to be working at this level of law. But soon I discovered my day-to-day assignments involved facilitating ways to assure the smooth running of huge corporations, regardless of the costs, emotional or economic, imposed on those with less power. Around that time, reports began coming out about the dark history of Hanford's role in the poisoning of thousands of "downwinders" in the Tri-Cities due to the inadequate measures that had been taken to contain radioactive emissions and to safely handle the storage of radioactive wastes.

People I had grown up with were victims of an emerging cancer epidemic. It seemed as if the residents in and around Richland, the Atomic City, were now residing in America's first Radioactive City. Previously secret studies about the health effects of Hanford's operations were coming to light that indicated that the government and its corporate partners had been engaged in a cover-up. I began to question seriously my place in what seemed to be the belly of the same beast as those who were running the Hanford operation.

Was I to become a Hanford cancer victim? Or my family members there? I thought about how much time I had spent swimming and water-skiing in the Columbia River, inevitably gulping down mouthfuls of its waters into which radioactive materials had been released. My fear of being a victim was replaced by my growing anger about the situation.

I reached a tipping point when I learned that several of the firm's senior partners were strong supporters of Ronald Reagan and had played an important part in his successful campaign in 1966 to become Governor of California. They were also members of Reagan's kitchen cabinet working to help him become the President of the United States, the so-called most powerful man in the world. I considered Reagan to be wholly unqualified.

One Friday night, I was sitting with a group of the firm's partners and associates having drinks in a dimly-lit bar near the office. It was a weekly ritual that offered an opportunity for us newer lawyers to socialize a bit with the partners, and up to that night I'd attended every one. We'd sit around a large table and talk about anything but work. On this night, one of the senior partners said as he rattled around the ice cubes in his drink, "We're going to go with this guy all the way to the White House. He's just smart enough, and just dumb enough to be managed and led to make the right decisions. Just look at the list of his judicial appointments so far. And mark my words, he is going to come down hard on the crap going on at the Berkeley campus."

One of the associates asked, "Which guy?"

To which the partner replied, "Reagan, of course."

Had I heard right? Reagan?! What the hell?!

To me, Reagan was the Borax Man in the TV ads, pushing household cleaning powder products. That and the smarmy movie actor who co-starred with a monkey.

As most of the others around the table nodded with varying degrees of interest or agreement, I thought to myself, "What nonsense is this coming out of the mouth of a person of supposedly sound judgment?"

This partner then recounted how the firm had worked to help Reagan become the governor and how they were going to help put him in the White House. I quietly excused myself and left, realizing that I really was in the belly of the beast and knowing I had to escape.

During my bus commute across the Bay Bridge that evening I recalled a comment that a Hollywood director had reportedly made when he was told of Reagan's presidential ambitions, "No, no, no! Charlton Heston as president; Reagan as his best friend."

I telephoned Pete McCloskey, my friend and mentor from my Stanford law school days, to bemoan the situation. He was a Republican but not a Reagan man, and he patiently listened as I spilled my guts. "Yeah, you made a bad choice in throwing in with that bunch. But I suggest you consider sticking around there for a bit. You're in a great spot to learn how these guys operate and to learn how to practice law as well as they do, so you can take them on successfully down the road."

It was good advice, and I took it. It was far from easy to continue my work at the firm, but Pete was right about learning how to practice law in high gear. I kept my political views to myself, and I could tell that I was seen as a future partner. I formed a warm bond and an excellent working relationship with Doug Hughmanick, one of the firm's senior partners and top trial lawyers, to whom I expressed my misgivings about remaining at the firm. He was not one of the firm's politically-active lawyers, and he understood my predicament.

At the Thelen firm, we associate attorneys worked primarily for two senior partners. Besides Doug, I worked for a partner who was almost perfectly described in a book titled *Confessions of an Economic Hitman* that came out years later. The author describes what he calls a system of corporatocracy in which America's most powerful corporations worked hand in glove with the United States National Security Agency to corner the leaders of developing nations into doing business with them on terms favorable to American economic and political interests.

The Thelen partner was part of the firm's Reagan cabal, he loved his work and the life it afforded, and he had marked me out as his possible successor when he retired in a few years. He expected me to respond with great enthusiasm to such a prospect, and when I didn't, he reacted with suspicion. One day he said, "Aren't you the Hanford and Stanford guy? Why do you still live in a place like Berkeley, for God's sake?"

Events that took place on the moon on Christmas Eve in 1968 opened the way to resolving my dilemma. On that date, the astronauts of the

"Earthrise" from Apollo 8, December 24, 1968. *Photo by Bill Anders/NASA.*

Apollo 8 lunar mission snapped one of most remarkable photographs ever taken and immediately transmitted it to the Houston Control Center back on Earth. I first saw it a week later, projected on the huge screen of a lecture auditorium on the Berkeley campus near my home. It knocked me for a loop.

It was a view of the Earth as seen from outer space, the world-shaking Earthrise image of the planet rising above the moon's gray horizon.

That night I fell head over heels in boundless love. The sight took my breath away, overwhelmed my thinking mind, and I felt as though I were floating in space, looking at the heavenly body from far, far above its surface. Partly in shadow, partly in light, day and night, the globe, all of the communities of life, all of the lives of the living, all of the past and the future that might be; it was all there.

It was utterly gorgeous and supremely holy. All the glimmerings of spiritual awareness that had been flickering in the background of my consciousness up until then came together in a burst of blinding white light. For the first time, I knew myself to be an Earthling living in and upon a whole new world, a world illuminated by Whole Earth consciousness.

Since then, I have always kept nearby a print of the Earthrise image to remind me of who I am and why I'm here. Something clicked into place that night. It made me see who I might be and what I might do. It truly was an awakening.

In early March of 1969, l got a phone call that set my life on a new course.

I was in my law office on the 11th floor at 111 Sutter Street, in San Francisco. A case file lay open on my desk, and I held my Dictaphone, just about to record some notes and correspondence, when my secretary buzzed over the intercom and said, "There's a Pete McCloskey from Washington, DC on the line for you."

I put down the recorder, reached for the telephone and heard Pete say, "Marc, have you heard about this oil platform blowout in Santa Barbara?"

"Hi Pete. Yes, I read some of the news about it."

"Well, I think you should get down there as quickly as you can and get involved. This is going to open up a whole new field of law. I'm at work right now helping to draft new legislation that will fundamentally change how governmental decisions affecting the environment are made. Young lawyers like you are going to be needed to enforce it in the courts. It's a National Environmental Policy Act, and we want to be sure that similar state laws are enacted and enforced."

"Yes, but..."

"No 'buts' about it, Marc. No time to waste. Get down there as soon as you can. Let Doug (Hughmanick) know and call me tomorrow. That's all for now."

I put down the phone, opened my arms to the heavens and whooped. I crossed the room to the window, opened it and shouted "Yes!" to the skyline. When I turned around, my secretary was staring at me with a mixture of alarm and astonishment. I told her I'd tell her all about it after I had spoken to Mr. Hughmanick.

That night Kathy and I talked it over and decided to make the move. The next morning, I met Doug in his office to tell him of my decision;

One of the beaches covered in oil from the 1969 Santa Barbara oil blowout.
Photo courtesy of Bud Bottoms.

Santa Barbara oil blowout on Platform A, January 28, 1969. *Photo courtesy of US National Archives via Wikimedia Commons.*

he smiled and said, "This opportunity is just right for you," and then I called Pete.

Pete asked, "Do you know anybody down there, Marc? Do you have any contacts with any lawyers?"

"No. Not a soul."

"Well, start as soon as you can. I'll see what I can do. But I want to let you know, this is really important. We need to make sure that the word coming out of Santa Barbara is stronger than just 'get oil out!' The bigger goal is to launch a powerful environmental protection movement across the whole country."

Pete McCloskey was then and still is (going strong at age 90) an Earthangel, the first of many with whom it has been a blessing to work with over the years to create and sustain such a movement.

The blowout at Union Oil's Platform A occurred on January 28, 1969, and in response, the citizens of Santa Barbara were angry as hornets. They had every right to be.

Before the offshore rigs were built, the locals had called for public hearings concerning the safety issues inherent to this kind of oil production. Those requests for hearings were denied by federal officials, who were in a rush to get started. The oil companies had paid millions of dollars to the federal government for the leases and, as Stewart Udall (Secretary of the Interior under Kennedy and Johnson) later explained, the government urgently needed those lease fees to help pay for the Vietnam War.

So, Udall looked the other way as the oil companies moved aggressively forward with these offshore rigs, and ultimately it was Udall (undoubtedly at the direction of the president) who made the decision to approve drilling operations. That decision was premature, as the events of late January demonstrated.

The blowout, which spewed more than three million gallons of crude oil and gas into the Santa Barbara Channel, occurred when the drill being operated from the platform penetrated to a depth that was not protected by the casing needed to contain the pressure of the materials below. The oil came exploding out, reached the surface and began to spread.

Dead bird from the 1969 Santa Barbara oil spill. *Photo courtesy of Bud Bottoms.*

It continued to spread over the next several months. Winds and tide moved it about, and soon it spread all along the shores of the South Coast. Sea life was deeply impacted. Birds who lived on the water were coated in oil, rendering them helplessly unable to fly or dive.

The birds became emblematic of the disaster because they generated the most compelling images. Poignant scenes of oil-covered birds helped to make the spill a national media event carried by major news organizations into the homes of people across the country.

As the efforts to stop the spill failed, the damage continued and so did the news coverage. At that point in time it was the largest water pollution incident in United States history. This created a new national awareness of environmental abuse and set into motion seminal laws, policy, and a change in social consciousness.

In that moment, journalism served well its role as the fourth estate. There were several prominent journalists covering the event at *The New York Times, The Chicago Tribune* and *The Los Angeles Times.* Locally, Bob Sollen covered the spill for *The Santa Barbara News-Press*, performing at the hub of this seminal event and briefing the national newspapers, sharing his photographs and accounts.

In addition to portraying the environmental devastation, the news media also covered representatives and dignitaries who visited the scene of the disaster. President Nixon arrived by helicopter, stepped out near

President Richard Nixon surrounded by media at a Santa Barbara beach, 1969.
Photo courtesy of Richard Nixon Presidential Library and Museum [Public domain],
via Wikimedia Commons.

the black gunk that had come ashore, and took pains to avoid sullying
his wingtip shoes in the grime.

Nixon was soon followed by Secretary of the Interior Walter
Hickel and a whole host of other federal and state government officials who showed up to sternly deplore the situation. Press releases
came out of governmental offices, and reporters diligently covered
the saga. For months, visiting representatives and the national
media audience watched the angry citizens of Santa Barbara vent
their fury at the federal officials who had ignored their warnings
and betrayed their trust.

The new National Environmental Policy Act (NEPA) that Pete had
mentioned would require developers to assess the environmental impacts
of their projects in advance and submit this information for public review
and potential court approval before moving forward. Had this requirement been in effect prior to the government's approval of the plan to

begin drilling operations in the Santa Barbara Channel, the blowout on Platform A would almost certainly have been avoided.

At the time Kathy and I decided to move to Santa Barbara, she was pregnant and our financial resources were thin. But in light of my having fallen in love with the Earth, as well as with her, we knew it was exactly what we should do. In a way, our son's gestation was part of my new way of seeing things. I was ready to defend the Earth. Within days of the birth of our son Skye, we moved to Santa Barbara.

Seizing the Moment

3

The challenge of finding a new job as a lawyer in Santa Barbara while living in San Francisco in the pre-internet age wasn't as easy as it would be today. I used the Yellow Pages phone directory and made a bunch of cold calls to random firms. "Hello, my name is Marc McGinnes. I'm in San Francisco with the firm of Thelen, Marrin, Johnson and Bridges. Yes, the Thelen firm. I'm planning on coming to Santa Barbara, and I would like to come by your office for an interview at your earliest convenience."

In this way I got a few affirmative responses, set up interviews and drove down to meet with prospective employers. I couldn't afford to hop on a plane.

I became an associate attorney with the Santa Barbara law firm of Westwick, Collison & Talaga. Before accepting their offer, I told them that the primary reason I was coming to town was to be a part of the response to the oil platform blowout and spill. In addition to my work for the firm, I told them that I intended to devote considerable time to this community-centered work.

Jim Westwick, the firm's senior partner, said, "Well, you'll be glad to know we are creating a nonprofit corporation for a group of notable folks who want to take court action to prevent further offshore oil operations. They are called the Santa Barbara Citizens for Environmental Defense. I will help you to meet these folks. They have big plans, and I think they will be interested in meeting you."

That sealed the deal.

The legal scene in Santa Barbara was far more laid-back and slow-going than the intense, high-speed one in which I had gotten my legal wings in San Francisco. My training at the Thelen firm couldn't have been better for the new fight at hand. I knew what it was like to work with highly effective lawyers on behalf of very powerful corporate interests. I had an insider's sense of exactly who we were up against, what their arsenal was and how to proceed against them. I felt confident that I could handle any legal issues that would be involved down the line.

But I certainly didn't know my way around in my new community, and for starters I had no clue about where to live. I found a fairly decent place pretty quickly in Isla Vista, next to the University of California, Santa Barbara (UCSB) campus. When the partners at my new firm found out, they were shocked. "You really can't live in Isla Vista. It is for students, not for attorneys. Montecito, the Riviera, Mission Canyon are areas where attorneys have their homes down here. We'll get some of our real estate people to get you right out of there." I caught their drift and soon found a sweet spot in Santa Barbara near the County Bowl.

The day I walked out of my office in San Francisco, I began to grow my hair long and tried out a moustache as well. When I showed up for work my first day in Santa Barbara I did not look like the short-haired, clean-shaven man I had been when I interviewed for the job. Jim asked me to please get a haircut and shave off the moustache, and I did.

The stench from the oil on the beaches hung heavily in the air. I was not about to let the length of my hair become a distraction in working for the firm's clients and with members of the community in order to respond to the oil pollution disaster in a manner that could launch a national environmental protection movement, which was the intention.

Governmental and corporate indifference to environmental abuse affected communities all across the country and around the world. Santa Barbara was a particularly vivid case in point, and the response of the Santa Barbara community could mark a turning point in helping people everywhere—Earthlings all, regardless of place or race—to confront and overcome environmental indifference and abuse affecting the health, safety and welfare of people everywhere.

In June of 1969 the heavily-polluted Cuyahoga River in Cleveland caught on fire. How could such a thing as a burning river ever happen? In what community might such a thing happen again?

Where might another oil platform blowout and oil pollution disaster take place? Or an oil tanker run aground, as the *Torrey Canyon* had along the coast of the United Kingdom in 1967? Where might a nuclear reactor irradiate its surroundings as the ones at Hanford had done and continued to do?

Might the cumulative effects of environmental abuses in places all over the Earth come to imperil all life on the planet by altering the conditions of even the oceans and the atmosphere?

Having seen the Earth from outer space, these were the kinds of questions on my mind as I began my environmental work in Santa Barbara. Having seen the whole Earth, I had been nudged into thinking holistically. As an environmental lawyer I believed my "clients" to be my fellow Earthlings everywhere, including future generations of human beings and all of the other communities of life on the planet.

The Santa Barbara Citizens for Environmental Defense (SBCED) board of directors were interested in filing lawsuits to obtain a court order to stop all oil drilling operations in the Santa Barbara Channel, pending full public hearings to consider and review relevant geological and other conditions and required safety precautions. The directors were Robert O. Easton, Kenneth Millar, Norman K. Sanders (an associate professor at UCSB), W. H. "Ping" Ferry and Selma Rubin.

Some of CEC's board members and advisors at El Mirasol (left to right), Bob Easton, John Smith, Maryanne Mott, Selma Rubin, Carla Frisk, unidentified, Joan Crowder, unidentified, Elaine Burnell and unidentified. *Photo courtesy of Community Environmental Council Archive, UCSB Library Special Collections.*

At the opening of the Ecology Center on Earth Day 1970. From left to right: Pearl Chase, County Supervisor George Clyde, Elaine Burnell and Marc McGinnes. *Photo courtesy of Community Environmental Council Archive, UCSB Library Special Collections.*

Ping was the vice president of the Center for the Study of Democratic Institutions, the think tank up on Eucalyptus Hill Road, which had been founded by Robert Hutchins, former University of Chicago president. Because of SBCED's relationship to my new firm, I met all of these movers and shakers immediately upon my arrival.

It was a really intelligent and stimulating crowd, and I threw myself headlong into their work. But SBCED was just one part of the landscape of institutions into which I had stepped. Other involved groups included the Sierra Club, the Audubon Society, the Citizens Planning Association, the League of Women Voters, Pearl Chase's organization Santa Barbara Plans and Planting and crucially, Get Oil Out! (GOO!).

Under the leadership of Bud Bottoms, State Senator Al Weingand, Lois Sidenberg, John Schaff and many others, GOO! channeled the anger visibly on television screens and front pages nationwide, transforming it into political action at the level of ordinary citizens. GOO! circulated petitions within the community and beyond, gaining tens of thousands of signatures addressed to government representatives, demanding the cessation of further oil operations in the Santa Barbara Channel.

GOO! volunteers gathering petition signatures, 1969. *Photo courtesy of Bud Bottoms.*

The news media allowed them to connect with a national audience, newly concerned about issues of pollution in their own communities. The circulation of these petitions and other materials took place without the ease of the internet age. Copy machines were in their infancy, and people had to make carbon copies and mimeographs, spread them via good old-fashioned postal mail, and post them by hand onto billboards and walls.

Laden with the signatures of people from across the nation, the petitions were carried to Washington, DC by the Santa Barbara citizens in the group with greatest influence. Lois Seidenberg of GOO!, a beautiful equestrienne and a woman of means, really knew how things worked in Washington. She felt comfortable walking into anyone's office, including the president's, to demand a moment of time and attention.

Our congressman, Charles Teague, a Republican then in his seventh term and hardly an environmentalist, was in the hot seat. His constituents besieged him everywhere, demanding that he pass along GOO!'s and other anti-oil petitions and that he take a forceful leadership role. The slogan "If the people lead, the leaders will follow" applied to Teague, and he was led to do more than he really wanted to do, and that was unsettling to his friends and supporters in the oil industry.

Bud Bottoms posing with a pile of dead birds he collected after the Santa Barbara oil spill, 1969. *Photo courtesy of Bud Bottoms.*

Bud Bottoms was the co-founder of GOO!, and he created the group's graphics and publicity. An extraordinarily talented artist and illustrator, Bud wrote and illustrated a children's book, *Davey and the GOM*, featuring an oil-covered boogeyman (GOM stood for Giant Oil Monster) who was confronted and overcome by a youngster's Santa Barbara-like community.

Davey and the Giant Oil Monster by Bud Bottoms. *Image courtesy of Bud Bottoms.*

The technology did not then exist to move at a speed much faster than a walk when it came to circulating petitions, letters and images. By today's standards, it was like traveling through molasses, in terms of the time and effort required to share ideas with others.

Since I was such a recent arrival, some people were skeptical of my motives, thinking I might be an opportunistic carpetbagger seeking political position or financial gain of some sort. Others saw that I had good intentions and powerful allies, and they positioned me to do the most good. One of those people was SBCED's co-founder, Robert O. Easton.

Bob Easton—in company with Dick Smith, Ian McMillen, Ken Millar and Jim Mills—established the San Rafael Wilderness, the first Wilderness Area in the United States after the 1965 Wilderness Act was adopted.

Bob sized me up quickly. The fact that Pete McCloskey had sent me and that Paul Ehrlich had been my advisor at Stanford gave me a lot of credibility. Bob and I were allies and friends almost immediately. He recognized that my being a newcomer actually suited me to assume

Bob Easton. *Photo courtesy of Joan Easton Lentz.*

leadership in a way that avoided the ego issues that sometimes arise in ongoing relationships.

He listened intently when I described an idea that had come to me and a group of neighbors a few days earlier. We thought that many prominent leaders from government, education and nonprofit groups would be willing to pay their own way to come to Santa Barbara on the first anniversary of the oil platform blowout to take part in what would be the first national conference on the environment. We thought the timing would be perfect. We called ourselves ECO-Collective. Its members were Russ and Marguerite Waldrop, John and Della Meengs, Paula Kelly, Don Watanabe, Warren Pierce and Kathy and I.

Bob responded enthusiastically to the idea, and he promptly convened a meeting of the SBCED directors to discuss it. The other directors expressed strong support, and it was agreed that SBCED would offer to take a leading part in the effort. Bob asked me if I would be willing to head up this effort, and I was subsequently selected as Chair of the January 28 Committee.

Bob knew that I wouldn't be able to assume the role of chairman without receiving the approval of community leader Pearl Chase. Within a month or two of my arrival in Santa Barbara, he arranged for me to meet Ms. Chase at her house, so that she could decide whether I was a person worthy of her and the community's trust.

Ms. Chase was eighty years old at the time, and just three years older than I am at the time of this writing. She had been quite a force in the community. More than any other individual, she is responsible for the Spanish colonial look of Santa Barbara as we know it: the white stucco, the red tile roofs, and the abundance of greenery, all legacies of her vision for our city.

The Santa Barbara earthquake of 1925 had destroyed many buildings and presented an opportunity for city planning based on a more unified community look. Pearl Chase seized this opportunity. Her influence didn't derive from being elected, but she understood how to create and wield power in institutions, and she became an institution herself. I was somewhat afraid of meeting with her, as I'd been told that she'd once stormed into the mayor's office, took him by his necktie and scolded him for taking an action she didn't approve of.

Pearl Chase. *Photo courtesy of Santa Barbara Historical Society.*

I embarked on my pilgrimage to Ms. Chase's house in the early morning. I straightened my tie with clammy palms, hoping she wouldn't have occasion to use it as a handle. A maid opened the door, and I saw that there was an entryway opening upon a sunroom. The bright light was streaming into the hallway and it backlit a small figure I knew at once to be Ms. Chase.

Blinded by the sun, I couldn't see her, but I knew she could see me. She stood there looking at me for what felt like an eternity, while I squinted and sweated. Finally, she said, "Well, come in, young man!"

I wondered if that was supposed to be welcoming, or if she thought I was an idiot. Quite frail and bent over, with white hair, Ms. Chase's gaze was both calm and piercing. I could see she didn't suffer fools. She turned and I followed her to two facing chairs placed close together. Sunbeams fell between them, motes floating lazily in the light.

When we were seated, she said, "What exactly brings you to town, young man?"

I told her about my friendship with Pete and his call to me, and she nodded at his name. Each time I mentioned Pete, she nodded again, so I had "Pe…" on my lips when she said. "I know all about Mr. McCloskey, young man. It's not him that I want to know about; it's you!"

So I told her everything, as she conducted an interrogation so searching yet courteous that one might have mistaken it for light conversation. It seemed then and seems now all these years later that Pearl Chase had benevolently hypnotizing powers.

At last she said, "And what about politics?"

I said that I had heard about but not yet met Gary Hart, the young Santa Barbara High and Stanford graduate who many people were urging to run for Congress or state office, and I said that I looked forward to helping him and others like him get elected.

"And you? What would you like to get elected to?" she asked.

"I don't want to get elected to anything."

"Good. You may find that you can get more done that way."

"So!" she said, rising from her chair, the word and the gesture letting me know that our meeting had come to a satisfactory conclusion. "Now, I've got things to do and I'm sure you do, too, having just arrived. I believe you have a lot on your plate. So, let me say good morning to you, young man. And good luck."

I had my marching orders. With this blessing, I was able to maintain the great confidence and passion I had in my purpose.

I had thought that Ms. Chase might not approve of me. My hopes would have been dashed on the spot had she judged me to be a carpetbagging interloper. Later I learned that Bob Easton had already spoken to Ms. Chase and voiced his vote of confidence in me.

Building the Movement

4

Ie held no banquet or celebration after the Environmental Rights Day Conference was over, and no awards or laurels were distributed that might have tempted any of us to rest upon. We had too much to get on with. The energy that had been crackling through the community throughout 1969 had come into focus and was increasing in intensity, undiminished by success.

It was from Paul Relis that I first heard the idea of creating an Ecology Center. Paul had been introduced to me by both Bud Bottoms and Bob Easton (within an hour of each other) a few weeks before the conference. Each told me that they thought Paul might have the answer to the question that we and other members of the January 28 Committee had been thinking about for awhile: where to take things when the conference was over?

When I met him, Paul Relis was exactly what he is to me today: an old soul in a far younger body. I saw then and still can see his glow.

Paul Relis at the Community Environmental Council in the early 70s. *Photo courtesy of Community Environmental Council Archives, UCSB Library Special Collections.*

Geodesic dome in CEC's El Mirasol gardens, 1970s. *Photo courtesy of Community Environmental Council Archive, UCSB Library Special Collections.*

Paul told me that people he knew had opened an Ecology Center in a storefront location in San Francisco that included a bookstore, reading room, meeting space and office equipment. He need not have said more, but since I enjoyed listening to his enthusiastic words, I kept still until he asked me what I thought about starting such a center in Santa Barbara.

"Let's get started right now!" I think I said, my mind running to consider creating the institutional framework for such an operation. An educational and community-benefit nonprofit corporation, I figured.

The final meeting of the January 28 Committee had one item of new business: to go out of business as an unincorporated association and to become a nonprofit corporation under the name Community Environmental Council (CEC).

I drew up the articles of incorporation and the tax exemption papers, and I became the founding president. John Meengs of the ECO-Collective was vice president and Selma Rubin was secretary-treasurer. Paul Relis was designated as the executive director.

Interior of Ecology Center, 1970. *Photo courtesy of Community Environmental Council Archive, UCSB Library Special Collections.*

We found an ideal downtown storefront location for the Ecology Center at 15 W. Anapamu Street, and I negotiated a long-term lease on it with the community-spirited owner who gave us a substantial break on the rent. Right next door at this time was the famous Henning's cake shop, and people with sweet teeth were among the Center's most frequent visitors after we opened our doors. Soon the place was packed.

We held the grand opening of the Ecology Center on the first Earth Day on April 22, 1970. Pearl Chase and County Supervisor George Clyde, the community's leading environmentalist in elective office, were the guests of honor.

The street was closed on the block in front of the center, and a very large and beautiful geodesic dome was erected there amidst tables and displays set up by various community groups and schools. All day long crowds milled about. The new green and gold ecology flag was unraveled. Lots and lots of bubbles blew in the air. Many important contacts were made. The acoustic musical performances were exceptionally fine.

The Ecology flag that flew at the Community Environmental Council.
Photo courtesy of Bud Bottoms.

We published *The Survival Times*, a newspaper that came out every couple of weeks, edited by Larry Penny. Larry Tower, Katey O'Neill and Hal Conklin were among its contributors. We made sure the meeting space was open to community groups and environmental organizations like the Sierra Club, Audubon Society, Scenic Shoreline Preservation and others, so that people could come together in a comfortable, centrally-located space and not have to rely on the availability of someone's private home or office.

We also used our location to facilitate a kind of activist matchmaking service between individuals and the groups to which they could most effectively lend their support, depending on their particular interest in organic gardening, wilderness preservation, shoreline preservation, community planning and so on.

It had always been important to Paul that we get our hands dirty and spread the gospel of organic gardening and farming. Not far away, there was a vacant plot of land near the bus depot at the corner of Chapala and Figueroa. I negotiated a lease with the generous owner, Miles Standish. We paid a token one dollar a year to use it.

Hal Conklin. *Photo courtesy of Community Environmental Council Archive, UCSB Library Special Collections.*

On this space, with the assistance of wonderful volunteers, we planted a diverse and colorful organic garden. As an attention-getter, it was pure magic. It really made people's eyes pop and stimulated their interest and questions. It was there that I came to love being a participant in the life that goes on in a garden. I'm happy to report that I have a green thumb.

In time, Hal Conklin (later to become city mayor) joined Paul as co-executive director, and the CEC shifted into a range of higher gears in order to undertake several important tasks in the community and beyond, including planning and operating the city's recycling program.

Over the years CEC has been a national and international leader in its areas of focus. Under the executive direction of Paul, Hal, Jon Clark, Bud Laurent, Bob Ferris, Dave Davis and Sigrid Wright, the CEC has attracted the support and active participation of a remarkably gifted group of women and men who have served as advisors and/or on its board of directors. Among a very long list of these are Dennis Allen, Jordan ben Shea, Diane Boss, Elaine Burnell, Laura Capps, Jeff Carmody, Oscar Carmona, Jon Clark, Joan Crowder, Charles Eckberg, Bob Fitzgerald, Carla Frisk, Jim Gildea, Dick Jensen, Ivor John, John Jostes, Kim Kimbell,

Bob Klausner, Phil Marking, Richard Merrill, Maryanne Mott, Mike Noling, Jack Overall, Detlev Peikert, Warren Pierce, John Smith, John Steed, Larry Thompson, Dennis Thompson, Susan Van Atta, Elizabeth Wagner, and Sally Warner-Arnett.

My tenure as Community Environmental Council president was brief, ending after less than two years, as my marriage to Kathy had fallen apart and I had to attend closely to personal matters.

My sadness at having to leave was tempered by my certainty that CEC was in highly capable hands and would continue to flourish. A few years ago CEC's directors

Bob Klausner. *Photo courtesy of Community Environmental Council Archive, UCSB Library Special Collections.*

made me a director emeritus, and it is a great honor for me to serve this wonderful organization, soon to be in its 50th year, in an informal advisory capacity today.

Adequate environmental protection required the recognition that pollution was not the only issue, but that the citizens needed to step forward and take control of the community planning process. We couldn't confine our activity to piecemeal action on the streets because the work wasn't just about protesting. Protesting was only one manifestation of citizens taking charge of their environmental rights and responsibilities. We wanted to empower people and provide ongoing opportunities to exercise those rights, in order to steer our democracy away from environmental indifference and abuse. Part of this involved recognizing how abuse could take place without a big dramatic event like the oil spill to grab public attention.

The community's reaction to the oil spill had been nearly unanimous and bipartisan. Everybody was on the same page about not wanting oil on

McKinley School students at the CEC garden, 1970s.
Photo courtesy of Community Environmental Council Archive, UCSB Library Special Collections.

the beaches. But when it came to other issues about which environmentalists were concerned, it was a different story.

As was the case in nearly all of Southern California at the time, Santa Barbara City and County political leaders were of a strongly pro-growth bent and catered to real estate development interests, such as those who banded together to resist a carefully planned approach to the creation of the Isla Vista student community next to UCSB.

These interests profited mightily from county policies which resulted in grossly overcrowded and underserved student communities that until relatively recently served as a textbook case of the consequences of poor planning driven by greed.

The character and pace of new residential and commercial development in the city and in other parts of the County of Santa Barbara had long been a matter of contention and maneuvering, but when Pearl Chase and others won a battle in 1968 against wealthy backers who wanted to construct high-rise, high-density residential towers on the site of what is now the Alice Keck Park Memorial Gardens, war seemed to break out. These backers were very bitter about their defeat, and they attempted to destroy Ms. Chase's citizens planning group, Santa Barbara Plans and Planting.

Ms. Chase wasn't having it, and she and her many old and new allies rallied to confront developers unwilling to confine their development expectations to fit within community standards. Of special importance in upholding community planning standards was, and remains today, the Citizens Planning Association, founded by Ms. Chase and others in 1960.

To me the environmental movement was nothing less than a Whole Earth liberation movement, and I knew that our resounding calls on Environmental Rights Day and Earth Day would engender a fierce backlash from entrenched economic and political forces whose policies and practices we sought to undermine and overcome. Practically on cue, the alarm was sounded in 1971, calling upon right-thinking Americans to reject the communistic calls of environmentalists to re-think the nation's cultural, economic and political course.

In that year, Lewis F. Powell, Jr, later to become a Justice of the United States Supreme Court, wrote a memorandum to an official of the United States Chamber of Commerce warning its members of what was at stake if most people in the United States followed the environmentalist path: he saw environmentalism as a threat to free-market capitalism. He lumped environmentalists and consumer activists like Ralph Nader in the same camp as communists. For many months this memo was secretly circulated among titans of industry and their lobbyists and political prostitutes. Finally, it was leaked to Jack Anderson, a leading journalist-muckraker of the time, and battle lines began to be drawn.

I was called a communist a few times when I appeared before groups to talk about environmental law and the lessons of ecology. Once or twice a spicy adjective refined the caller's meaning as an insult, as if I could be provoked into lowering the discussion to a self-defeating level. In solidarity with my hero Pearl Chase, I smiled and soldiered on.

I could understand why what I was saying pissed off some people so much. The message that I was delivering did sound communistic to certain ears. What they thought they heard me say was, "Look here, you private property owners; your rights are less than the community's rights to protect and promote the public, health, safety and welfare. Which means that your property rights are far from absolute and can be regulated within reasonable limits, including for the purpose of protecting the environment."

One fellow opined in a letter to the editor of a local newspaper that I ought to "go to Moscow."

I pointed out that what he thought he heard me say was not a communist party line, but were in fact the very words used by the Supreme Court in a landmark case concerning the limits placed upon private property rights by the United States Constitution.

 And yet these were the days when you would come across billboards demanding "Impeach Earl Warren!" against the Chief Justice of the United States Supreme Court. It was a time of determined resistance to the recognition of the civil rights of minorities of all kinds. My task was to fight for the recognition by the majority of citizens that their civil rights extended to their protection from "environmental indifference and abuse." It seemed to me to be a worthy cause, and I was grateful to be engaged on the front lines of the struggle.

Little by little we were chipping away at the notion that "you can't fight City Hall" when it came to confronting policies and practices that were detrimental to the public interest, and little by little we began to elect candidates who would comprise the majority of the members of the City Council and other elected decision-making bodies.

All this community involvement took place during my "spare time," while I continued working for the Westwick law firm. For a short period after the conference, my bosses were delighted that I was becoming well known in the community and was bringing in new clients to the firm. They weren't environmental clients specifically, just people responding to my new name recognition. I took great care, as I had learned to do with my prior firm in San Francisco, to keep meticulous records of the time I was devoting to work for the Westwick firm (my "billable hours") to make it clear that they were getting their money's worth for the salary they were paying me. My environmental work was done on my own time, and the time I devoted to it exceeded my billable hours for the firm.

As I worked long hours in order to juggle successfully my professional, familial, and community responsibilities, I began to consider the prospect of leaving the Westwick firm and opening up my own office as a "sole practitioner." I figured that I would be able to cut back on the forty plus hours I was working at the firm and still be able to earn as much or more income working on my own. Importantly, I would also have control over the number of hours I had to work for paying clients to make ends meet.

My decision to go out on my own was precipitated—sooner than I had expected—by what I considered to be a shameful decision by the Westwick firm. They chose to take Jules Berman as a client in order to assist him in obtaining approval of a plan for a high-density residential development of fifteen hundred thirty-five homes on undeveloped land at El Capitan Ranch on the Gaviota Coast, effectively expanding Goleta.

I informed the three partners of the firm that I believed it was a clear conflict of interest to take on Berman when the firm already represented a client, Santa Barbara Citizens for Environmental Defense (SBCED), that would obviously oppose such a plan.

The heat in my office shot up as we stood staring hotly at one another. I saw dollar signs glinting in their eyes and realized they were not going to change their minds. I silently opened each drawer of my desk and began placing items on the surface. I gathered and stacked manila folders on the edge. I walked past the trio to my bookcase and removed pictures from the top and a few of the books from the shelves. I placed a few of these items in my briefcase, and bent over my desk to write "boxes" on a slip of paper which I slipped into a pocket.

"I quit," I said, "and I will be taking my client, SBCED, with me."

When one of the partners tried to interject, I raised my hand to cut him off, but he stepped close to me and said through gritted teeth, "You had better take no action as a lawyer in connection with the El Capitan case. If you do, we will aggressively pursue charges of conflict of interest on the grounds that you were a member of this firm at the time it represented Berman."

Had we been in high school, maybe even in college, I almost certainly would have punched him hard squarely on the nose. As it was, I moved around him and left the three of them shuffling uncomfortably out of the room.

It was not this pathetic threat that kept me from taking a leading role in confronting the El Capitan development; it was the need to establish myself in my own law office as quickly as I could in order to bring in enough money to provide for my family. Even so, it was a great disappointment to have to take a sideline seat as the battle over El Capitan and the Gaviota Coast played out.

I set up my own office as a sole practitioner in the La Arcada building, a beautiful spot downtown. I remodeled the charming space myself and it felt so wonderful to be on my own. I had a sign carved, that read: J. Marc McGinnes Attorney and Counselor at Law! I knew I was on the right track. And I felt that I had taken a giant step forward in my plan to open a full-time public-interest environmental law firm to serve the community and the region.

I was becoming a Santa Barbarban. I grew my hair long again and got rid of all but a few suits and ties and went to my office in informal clothes. Happily, in the aftermath of the conference, I had enough clients to sustain myself.

I took what environmental law cases I could, but I had to pay my bills, so I was also doing divorces and other cases that came my way. I had all kinds of opportunities, if I'd been so inclined, to return to corporate law, or to be a small business lawyer, but those cases weren't interesting to me at all anymore. In time it was a great pleasure to refer many people seeking my service to my good friend Ken Falstrom who became my own personal lawyer as well.

Meanwhile, as the El Capitan case advanced, Frank Sarguis was hired to represent the opposition to the development. He was an excellent lawyer. Knowing that the case was in his good hands helped me through this extremely galling period.

My former firm succeeded in winning the approval of Berman's subdivision plans from the Planning Commission and the County Board of Supervisors. But the opposition used the referendum process, where you circulate a petition to the voters of the county, and if you get ten percent of those who voted in the prior general election to sign it, then the subject of the petition is placed onto the ballot in the forthcoming election to be decided by a majority vote.

As a private citizen I worked with Selma Rubin and many others to get the necessary signatures, and the issue came to a vote. By an overwhelming two-to-one margin, the voters of the county overturned the decision of the Board of Supervisors and rejected the development.

After this successful referendum, District Attorney Dave Minier and my former firm brought, respectively, criminal and civil charges against Selma Rubin and her friend Anna Laura Meyers. They were accused of intentionally mishandling the referendum petitions. They went to trial and were—unsurprisingly—acquitted of any wrongdoing.

The whole thing was just an effort to intimidate and discourage citizens from resisting development. If Selma and her fellow citizens had not taken action to prevent the El Capitan subdivision project, it would have led to the leapfrog development of the whole Gaviota Coast.

There's a bench in the El Capitan Campground honoring Selma for that work. Sitting on that bench today, I feel great gratitude for the work of all the individuals who struggled then and who continue to work today to protect that Gaviota coastline. I loved Selma. She was my eco-mom.

Speaking of unspoiled coastlines, Santa Barbara locals know the beautiful public open space and unofficial nude beach on the property commonly known as More Mesa, and they may recall something about the dramatic incidents in the early seventies, when it was nearly turned completely into a sprawling residential subdivision. The name of the proposed development was Tyrolian Village, and the architecture had a wildly inappropriate Alpine flair. The units were absurdly reminiscent of little ski chalets, built to withstand a heavy load of snow on their roofs.

The movement to oppose the development was led primarily by the Scenic Shoreline Preservation Committee, the Sierra Club, the Audubon Society and the Citizen's Planning Association. More Mesa was important open space and habitat, particularly for the White-tailed Kite, that beautiful bird that can hover so impressively in one place before diving to strike its prey on the ground. A great many people were opposed to the project because it would also block public access to the popular beach below the mesa.

The prospective developer was making efforts to shut down the traditional public use of More Mesa as open space and beach access. Over many years, I had made it known at the Board of Supervisors' hearings that the county needed to survey areas of public access, beaches and so forth, open to the public.

Selma Rubin, late 1970s. *Photo courtesy of Community Environmental Council Archive.*
UCSB Library Special Collections.

We needed this information because if there were places where
access had been open and continuous for a period of at least five years,
then those uses legally "ripen" into permanent public easements. This
rule of property law is called "implied dedication." It's a use-it-or-lose-it
scenario. If you don't use your right to exclude people, you can actually
lose the right forever. The public can actually gain rights by trespassing
if the owner doesn't successfully resist it. This drives property owners
crazy, but it's the law.

The doctrine of implied dedication applies to inland as well as coastal
property. We used it to prevent the closure of hiking trails in the mountains above Santa Barbara, and the law is especially important to prevent
attempted closures of trails along the coast that would block access to the
beaches. This is because the State Constitution provides that all beaches
in California seaward of the mean high tide belong to the public and not
to any adjacent landowner.

I was working in my office one day when I received a call from a
young woman who was choking back angry tears. She asked to come to
my office as soon as I could see her. When she arrived she told me she'd

just been assaulted out at More Mesa. Apparently, she and her girlfriend had been trying to go to the nude beach and were walking along the well-worn path when they were stopped by a uniformed rent-a-cop who told them they were trespassing and demanded that they leave immediately or be arrested. The two women said they knew they had a right to be there and informed him that they'd been coming to the beach a lot longer than he had been around. An exchange of profanity occurred, and the security guard started pushing them around.

She was furious at the way she'd been treated. We decided we'd go out there immediately to discuss the situation with him. We rode out together on my motorcycle, she behind me, holding me tight, hair blowing in the wind (this was before you had to wear a helmet). I have always loved riding motorcycles, and I ride one still.

The security guard was still there when we pulled up. He immediately began yelling at her and trotted towards us threatening to arrest her. He was about to grab her when I stepped in front of him and growled, "Don't touch her."

He shouted, "Who the hell are you?" I introduced myself and reached for my business card, but before I could, he puffed up to twice his already ample size and demanded we both get out of there or he would arrest both of us.

I said, "Wait, you don't seem to understand what's going on." He said that he did, and that's when he pulled his gun on me.

I was petrified, thinking, whoa, this is not going to be a good way to die, to be shot by an angry rent-a-cop right here on the spot. At that time in my life, I had not thought much about how I would prefer to die, but even if I had, I would not have imagined this way.

The woman screamed—at me!!—"Marc, don't!"

That brought the man up short, both of us wondering what the woman thought I was getting ready to do.

He took a few steps back and lowered his pistol. He seemed as dazed as I was by our close encounter. The woman said to him, "If you're going to call the sheriff, do it right now or we are leaving. This man is my lawyer."

That was not the advice I would have given her, but she had taken charge, and the guard did what he was told and called the sheriff.

In what seemed like no time at all a sheriff's car arrived and two deputies got out and approached. Before the deputies could get a word out the guard blurted, "I am executing a citizen's arrest on these two people, and I want you to…." He was cut off by one of the deputies, a man I had spoken with a few times around the courthouse during my appearances there on behalf of my clients. He raised his eyebrows at me, miming his question, "What the hell?" and asked the guard, "What is going on here?"

The deputy let the guard pour out his story, shook his

Marc dressed in his law office attire during the 1970s. *Photo courtesy of Marc McGinnes Archives.*

head in disbelief and asked, "You want to do a citizen's arrest on an attorney? Both an attorney and his client? Really?!"

In the silence that ensued you could hear the wind rustling through the tall grasses and I heard the screech of a hawk high above us. I asked the deputy who had just spoken to call the landowner's attorney, Stan Hatch, a man with whom I was friendly even though we were at odds where his clients were concerned.

When he came on the line, I said, "Stan, you won't believe what's going on out here. I just about got myself shot by the guard that you've got posted out here at More Mesa. I am here with my client whom the guard assaulted and battered when she and a friend were walking along the trail to the beach."

The silence at Stan's end was so deep and prolonged, that I was about to ask if he had heard me, when he replied. "Please call me when you get back to your office. I'd like to talk with whoever is there from the sheriff's office, please."

I handed the phone device to the deputy who had spoken to the guard, and I turned to leave with my client. Alas, she was still in charge. She took a step toward the guard, now reduced to something a good deal less than his normal size. I heard her hiss at him, "I will see you in court, mister!"

I have never heard those words spoken with more menace, not even in a movie.

I did file a lawsuit on her behalf against both the guard and Stan's client, and she was offered what I thought was a tidy sum to settle the case out of court. She balked a bit, wanting a piece of the guard's hide, but I told her that we had already won an important victory by getting Stan's agreement to have all guards removed from the site and to stop any efforts to interfere with beach access.

I advised her she would have to find another attorney if she wished to refuse the settlement and go to trial. She mulled on that for a moment and said, "We really did kick ass on them, didn't we? Okay, I'll take their offer. I can contribute the money to good causes, including stopping this awful project."

The terrible fact that we faced in opposing the project was that it was clear that three of the five members of the Board of Supervisors were strongly in the pro-growth political camp and were almost certainly going to approve it by a 3-2 vote. We would then have to seek to get a court to intervene, and I began to prepare for that. But then, something happened that was nearly beyond belief and that caused things to veer sharply in a different direction.

A few weeks before the Board was to meet and make its decision, my friend and neighbor Frank Frost who had recently been elected to the Board on a slow-growth platform, received a visit in his office from a fellow by the name of Phil Regan, a former Hollywood song and dance man who liked to rub elbows with conservative political leaders. Regan did not come to see Frank to rub elbows that day, but to see if he could grease his palm.

He told Frank that "there would be something in it" for Frank if he would vote in favor of the project and "something more" if he could get

Jim Slater, also recently elected to the Board on a slow-growth platform, to do the same. If the vote were to be 5-0 in favor of the project rather than 3-2, Regan said he thought opponents might not be able to rally support for a court challenge.

Frank told Regan that he'd think it over and invited him to return the next day. Frank then called the sheriff, described the situation, and agreed to wear a concealed listening device during the meeting with Regan.

Frank, a gifted jazz pianist and somewhat of a showman himself when he chose, gave a convincing performance of a greed-ball on the take. Regan offered to buy his vote and was arrested before he left the building. And the news was in all the papers and on the airwaves beginning the following day.

Just like that—snap!—it became too politically toxic for any of the three pro-growth supervisors to vote in favor of the project, and when the matter came before the board, the vote was 5-0 to deny it.

Attempts to purchase votes by out-and-out bribery are rare, but attempts by powerful interests to purchase votes by inducing elected decision-makers to act as political prostitutes are commonplace in the terribly skewed process of governance at the local, state and federal levels.

Political prostitution is allowed to flourish in a climate that enables powerful interests to lavish spending on the campaigns of people who are willing to accept money to win and retain their positions of power. What is needed is reform of the laws governing campaign contributions and spending whereby limits are imposed and enforced to prevent it.

The only other case of outright bribery that I have encountered during my career as a public interest environmental advocate occurred not long after the Tyrolian Village case. An administrative assistant to one of the county supervisors was caught and convicted and sent to jail when he accepted a cash offer to influence his boss's vote on a proposed development plan at Zaca Lake.

As is said, "Money talks," and citizens need to be vigilant in order to hold to account those in positions of public trust who are willing to listen and obey the siren call of greed.

Prior to the founding of the Environmental Defense Center, much of my private law practice involved helping people to navigate divorce proceedings and business disputes. I gained a reputation as a good person to come to when people wanted to avoid costly fights. By "costly" I mean the awful emotional as well as financial costs of allowing themselves to get caught up in the legal system's customary process of pitting one side *against* the other. The title that must be affixed to most court proceedings is "plaintiff(s) vs. defendant(s)." The term "vs." means "versus" and that means "against".

If we allow the inevitable conflicts that we all experience in our lives to be framed as contests between ourselves against others, we place ourselves in jeopardy. What we need to do is to frame our conflicts more realistically and healthfully. We can choose to look past the legal system's customary "plaintiff *vs.* defendant" formulation to see that our conflicts can be better understood and handled as matters of "plaintiff(s) *in re* defendant(s)". The term "in re" means "in relation to" and that signifies that *we are in relationship with those with whom we have differences.*

Here is a bit of wisdom about relationships: If you want to lose a relationship, do all you can to be the winning party in it.

What kind of life do we make for ourselves and our communities if the best we think we can do is to impose defeat on those with whom we experience the relationship of having differences?

At age 21, early in my first year of law school, I was startled to hear one of my professors declaim, "Conflict is a contest, and in order to win you have to do everything in your power to make the other side lose."

What the hell?! I raised my hand. The professor seemed irritated to be interrupted, but he allowed me to speak. I said something like, "sometimes conflict is a contest, but very often, it's not. If the legal system makes a contest out of most of our conflicts, doesn't it make our efforts to resolve them needlessly complex and expensive? Who 'wins' when this happens? Lawyers?"

I could have heard a pin drop, as he eyed me with a mixture of condescension and what? Respect? "Mr. McGinnes, you are in law school. The psychology department is somewhere else on campus. Are you sure that you are in the right place?"

I did not reply. I had my first inkling that I was, in fact, in the wrong place.

While the UC Berkeley law school was reputed to be among the best in the country, it seemed to me as I went on that it is more like a trade school. There was one course in jurisprudence, but it was open only to students in their second or third year. Of course, there was no course at all on the subject of mediation back in those days.

As a lawyer I learned about mediation by handling the kinds of cases that my clients brought with them through my door. The superiority of the principles and practices of mediation in helping my clients to work through their conflicts became obvious to me and to them. I gained a reputation for the way in which I sought to serve as an educator rather than a hired gun, and I was able to make my living in accordance with my values. The relatively modest fees that I received for my services were what sustained me as I continued to work with little or no compensation on environmental cases representing nonprofit groups with limited resources to pay me.

When my marriage to Kathy dissolved, we mediated our way through it. By doing so, we preserved our relationship, and today she is one of my dearest friends.

Of course, no amount of mediation can change the fact that the end of a marriage is a difficult time for all concerned, particularly when there's a child involved. Prior to the divorce, I'd been sailing along happily, blissfully in love with the Earth, and now it was as if I'd struck a wall, crushing my heart.

I passed my role at the CEC on to other leadership and tried to use this change in my life as an opportunity for spiritual growth and transformation. It was really a time for me to retreat and re-emerge as a stronger and more compassionate person.

Within a week or two of my arrival in Santa Barbara, I began a practice of meditation as taught by the Transcendental Meditation group that was then in town. Twice daily for 20 minutes I sat comfortably centering on a mantra, allowing thoughts to come and go, emptying busy-ness from my mind. It had a wonderful effect.

On the morning of the day I first met with the directors of the Santa Barbara Citizens for Environmental Defense, I emerged from my session in a state of alert receptivity that enabled me to handle the anxiety that might otherwise have gripped and distracted me. I felt no need to impress or to push my ideas. I knew my purpose in being among these good people, and I looked forward to listening and learning from them and to contributing what I could to the discussion.

Gradually my mediation practice evolved, and I moved into a deeply cleansing and refreshing practice of breathing inner light. I grew to meditate with my eyes open wide and my body in motion. And I meditated while lying on my back in the ocean, buoyant and cozy in my wetsuit. And I glided and flew in the water and performed yogic movements that cannot be done on land in the pull of gravity there.

I went rock climbing and hang gliding. I got Rolfed, I submitted myself to primal scream therapy (in my case it was more like primal yelling, and it left me hoarse), and I undertook a 28-day broth fast. The latter really confirmed my awareness that I am not confined within my body, but that my body lives in me.

One day, I found a piece of driftwood along the beach and carved into it the words "BOTH / AND" to symbolize my commitment to continue my journey free from the illusions of reductive either/or thinking. For forty years I kept that piece of wood within hand's reach, and during a recent move it seems to have chosen to move on, perhaps to the service of one in need. I am content that it be so.

As an environmental lawyer, I had a lot of educating to do. CEQA, the California Environmental Quality Act, was enacted in 1970 and was patterned after NEPA, the National Environmental Policy Act that Pete McCloskey had co-sponsored in Congress.

Both acts mandated an environmental impact review process, but CEQA was stronger than NEPA. I made it my business to know more than anybody about how these new laws would affect procedures at the local level. My early training prepared me to do the legal research needed. I learned about the law not so much to work as a trial advocate, but so I could serve as an educator to decision-makers and my fellow citizens.

I educated not only legal decision-makers like judges, but appointees and representatives on the Santa Barbara County Board of Supervisors, the Planning Commission, the City Council, and so on. In fact, most environmental law is practiced not in the courtroom, but in venues such as these, at an administrative level. In public hearings, citizens, experts and public interest attorneys can speak up in an open forum to remind decision-makers of their duties, informing them of the pertinent issues developers wouldn't care to raise, since these issues would be in opposition to the developers' own private interests.

Litigation is costly and time-consuming, and the proverbial "small group of thoughtful, committed citizens" is unlikely to have the resources for it. By contrast, public hearings provide a space where representation is relatively inexpensive and easy to navigate. Crucially, it's also a space where decision-makers are held accountable to their constituents in a very direct, open way, face to face and heart to heart.

The Harris Grade case was a perfect example of my work at educating decision-makers. It concerned the geography between Lompoc, Casmalia and Santa Maria. The proposal was to put in a road which would pass through an environmentally sensitive habitat. Local environmental groups were concerned, of course, and they proposed changing the route to prevent its destruction. The Road Department strongly objected, citing the added cost this would entail. The project required the approval of the Board of Supervisors, who prior to CEQA weren't required to consider environmental constraints on development.

I spoke at the public hearing on the proposal, explaining that the developers would have to hire an independent firm to conduct an environmental impact report and its findings would have to be taken into consideration before any decision could be made.

I then said that I had brought with me an expert witness to explain the nature and extent of the environmentally sensitive area.

One of the supervisors interrupted me, saying, "Just a minute, Mr. McGinnes. We really don't have to consider this."

"That's the point I've been making," I responded. "You have a duty to consider it. That's what the law requires of you now."

At that time, decision-makers just weren't aware of what the law now required of them and had to be informed. Versions of what was said in the Harris Grade were repeated in other cases before other decision-makers. To bring my message home strongly to them, I warned that we could sue them if they didn't comply with the law. "Don't take my word for it," I'd say. "Ask your legal advisers whether or not what I am saying is true."

Not all judges and public officials took kindly to my efforts to educate concerning their legal duties. One judge in particular took a very dim view of me and thought he would down me a notch or two. One day I came with my client for a routine procedure to wind up a dissolution of marriage case in which she and her husband had reached a full settlement of all issues. All that was required was for the judge to ask her to confirm the agreement and to enter an order to conclude the case.

We waited while the judge dealt with a few other matters. When the judge called our case, my client took her seat in the witness chair as I had directed and I stood in front of the judge's dais and began, "Your honor, we are here today to…"

The judge cut me off and growled, "Mr. McGinnes, I am not going to proceed with this matter until you see fit to appear in proper attire."

At this, I heard my client gasp, and I turned to her. She was staring wide-eyed at the judge and both of her hands covered her mouth. I turned to the judge whose expression was a ghastly mixture of triumph and disdain. In an even tone I said, "Wait just a minute. I stand before you properly attired in a suit and tie, and if you think you can…"

Again the judge cut me off and nearly rose from his chair as he summoned the court bailiff. "Bailiff," he bellowed, "remove this man from the courtroom!"

When he saw that I was about to speak, he said, "Mr. McGinnes, if you say one more word I will hold you in contempt of court and have the bailiff take you into custody!"

From some hitherto undiscovered place I was able to find sufficient strength to contain my rage and maintain a sufficient measure of self-control. I motioned to my client to rise from the witness chair and to accompany me out the door, the bailiff nipping at our heels.

In the hallway my client grabbed my arm and shouted. "That man is not fit to be a judge!"

The bailiff opened the door and gave her a threatening glare. She gave him the finger and went on in a lower voice full of fury, "This matter was about me and my life, not about what that fat-ass thinks about you or your attire."

The bailiff was listening at the door. I figured that she and I should walk away. We took a few steps, and then she stopped and said, "We are going down right now to the newspaper and tell them about this!"

And we did.

It was fairly early in the morning, and in those days the daily newspaper came out in the late afternoon.

On its front page that day was a picture of me and an accompanying article in which my client's comments about the judge and his unfitness and his disregard for her rights were prominently displayed. At the very end of the article was the single comment that the judge had "no comment" on the matter.

The event was far more life-changing for my client and the

FOR THIS ATTIRE, J. Marc McGinnes, attorney, was ousted from Superior Court today
—News-Press photo

Judge Ejects Lawyer From Courtroom for 'Improper Attire'

J. Marc McGinnes, an attorney, was ejected from Superior courtroom. When I again tried to make a brief statement the

Marc McGinnes inappropriately dressed for court, according to the judge, making the local news in his leather coat. *Image courtesy of The Santa Barbara News-Press.*

judge than it was for me. My client was soon enrolled in night-classes at the local law school from which she graduated in near-record time after which she promptly passed the bar exam, re-married, and became a successful and well-respected trial lawyer.

Things did not go nearly as well for the judge. Badgered by the horrible publicity he had called down on himself, he lost the support of many of the lawyers in town, some of whom liked to appear in court on Fridays wearing golf slacks (some in plaid!) below their coats and ties. When he was up for re-election, he had to mount a campaign—something that judges seldom have to do—to retain his seat, but he was soundly drubbed.

You may well wonder what the judge found improper about my attire. My client's theory was that the judge had leather issues, and that was what set him off: seeing that my sport coat was made of beautifully-worked soft leather rather than more modest cloth. She said she thought it looked good on me, and she laughed, "That man had no good judgment at all."

In those days, I traveled from hearing to hearing, educating, evangelizing, so to speak, spreading the good news. It was good news for the citizens' environmental groups because the new laws required decision-makers (even the most rabidly pro-growth ones) to take into careful consideration the environmental consequences of their decisions. Further, it mandated the denial of projects whose adverse environmental impacts could not be avoided or mitigated. In one fell swoop NEPA and CEQA fundamentally changed the decision-making process. In the Harris Grade case, this meant the decision was made to avoid plowing a road right through sensitive habitat.

The people had to learn about their new opportunities for participating in the governing process. I also educated them about the new responsibilities placed on government appointees and representatives. In a democracy, it's crucial that citizens understand not only their own duties, but the duties of government, so they can hold accountable those who govern. I gave guest lectures at UCSB, at SBCC, for the Kiwanis Club and other service organizations, the League of Women Voters, the Citizens' General Plan Committee, and in other public forums, educating citizens about the new environmental protection laws.

Ultimately, I also knew that in educating at the civic level I was laying the groundwork for the creation of a full-time public interest environmental law firm, because such a firm requires an educated constituency to work effectively. I was getting closer to creating the firm I had long dreamed of.

A Crisis of Relevance

5

In the late sixties and early seventies, higher education was facing a crisis of relevance. Colleges and universities struggled to address the social and environmental problems of the time. The academic field of Environmental Studies emerged from a new cultural awareness of environmental abuse. Peace Studies and Cultural Studies also emerged at this time. These developments were resisted by some conservative elements on campus, which marked them down as passing fads. But many educators had the right idea about environmental studies and its key component: ecology. They felt that this new interdisciplinary field could lead to a transformation of education across the board.

Because so much of my legal work was of an educational nature, it was no surprise to me that I also became an educator, in a more formal sense. This was due to my involvement in another of the many institutions germinated at this time, the Environmental Studies (ES) Program at UCSB.

After the oil spill, in 1970, a group of 21 faculty, calling themselves The Friends of the Human Habitat, met to discuss the possibility of promoting some form of environmental education at UCSB. They were geologists, geographers, engineers, biologists, an economist and

Logo of Introductory Environmental Studies Course (ES 1) taught by Marc.
Logo design by Steve Brown. *Image courtesy of Marc McGinnes Archives.*

a historian. The creation of Environmental Studies (ES) was spear-headed by Rod Nash, the charismatic history professor who drafted the Santa Barbara Declaration of Environmental Rights. Until this point in history the world of academia had not yet realized that it had overlooked a very important aspect of educating students on how to care for, respect, and develop a framework to protect our dynamically interconnected world.

Indeed, ecology itself had a transformative effect on education because it changed the way knowledge itself was conceived. At that time, they called ecology "the subversive science," because it's the science of relationships, not of discrete, bounded circumstances pertaining only to one part or another of the whole. The old approach to knowledge and science was (with few exceptions) a reductionist approach.

David Brower described the scientific reductionist approach with the metaphor of taking apart a clock. "If you're going to disassemble a clock to see how it works, you'd better keep track of all the pieces, keeping in mind that it takes all of them working in relation to each other to make the whole thing work. What is most important to observe and understand is how all of the parts work together in relationship. Focusing merely on the particular parts can be blinding."

An ecologist knows that if you try to sever or overlook a connection to the whole, you had better understand what you're doing, because the consequences will extend through all kinds of complex relationships with far-reaching implications.

Rod Nash was also aware that a program exploring ecology and ecological thinking would have to rely on a combination of knowledge from different fields, working in relationship. So, while at that time the concept of being interdisciplinary did not have the currency it does now—it would have been considered another airy-fairy idea by those same conservative elements that looked down upon Environmental Studies, Cultural Studies and Peace Studies—it was part of the vision for Environmental Studies at UCSB. ES would be a thoroughly interdisciplinary program, not a department centered around a single field of inquiry.

This was wise, because existing departments tend to worry about new departments stepping on their toes. To them a program was less threatening to a diversity of existing departmental resources such as joint faculty appointments. This was a great example of the wisdom of taking the "both/and" rather an "either/or" approach.

In drawing together these different groups, the program's founders had good allies. Nash worked with a strong committee of people to form the ES program. An important member of the founding group was Garrett Hardin, who was among the speaker lineup at the January 28 Conference, a professor widely respected for an article he had just written that explored what he called "the tragedy of the commons."

For many years Hardin's article was the most cited and discussed work in the field of ecology. The basic idea is that when you have a commons, an area where there are no private property rights, no one has the right to exclude any other persons from using it. So anyone can use it as she or he thinks fit. So let's say the commons is pasture where you and I can graze our cows. Since the livestock are our property while the pasture is not, each of us may decide to put as many cows on it as we like. If I put one cow, and you put one cow, and our neighbors all put one cow onto the commons to graze, everything may be fine so long as there is enough grass for all the cows to munch upon. But if you or I or our neighbors figure it would serve our self-interest to put several more, perhaps all of our cows, out to graze on the commons, what unintended consequence may ensue? What could possibly go wrong when we all make perfectly logical decisions about what's best for us as individuals?

Nothing will go wrong so long as there is enough grass. But what happens when the pasture can no longer provide grass for so many cattle—a point certain to arrive if we all continue to act in our self-interest. The pasture will have been damaged by overgrazing, and our cows will be facing starvation. It is an outcome that is harmful to each of us and to the land, individually and collectively.

Was this inevitable? Why or why not? What do you think? This will be on the exam at the end of the book.

Just kidding.

The tragedy is that individual self-interest and greed operates—without careful management through law or by other means—to destroy the commonwealth of communities and nations.

Is it not evident that this kind of conduct is a primary cause of the climate crisis and all of the environmental destruction caused by the so-called free-market system which enables those who capitalize for their own enrichment—so long as laissez-faire capitalism is tolerated—on the Earth's living systems?

True? False? Discuss and then take what action you deem appropriate. This is not an exam. This is real life. No kidding.

Rod asked me in 1970 if I would teach a course in environmental law for the new Environmental Studies Program at UCSB, and I began teaching there the following year. At the time I had my feet in two worlds, active law practice and teaching. I was working at the cutting edge of both making the law and teaching about it.

I taught the first Environmental Law course at UCSB, and although I had not previously thought seriously of teaching as my vocation, I really enjoyed it. It was called *Principles of Environmental Law: Personal and Planetary Perspectives*. I was allowed to do it my way, which meant I could discuss not only legal concepts with my students, but also the human priorities and moral duties of individuals living in a democratic system. It was philosophy. It was ethics. It encompassed everything.

I would say, "We don't need as much law as we need love. Let's talk about both here. Let's really get good at understanding the law, because it's a tool we want to master so we can guide it in the direction of love."

It was a rigorous course and I used the Socratic method to teach it rather than lecturing at the students. I invited my students to carefully consider the propositions that "law is us, but not just us" and "the law is up for grabs."

This led to interesting and fruitful conversations about the greedy and exploitive purposes to which laws can be put, or the loving and healing purposes to which laws can be put. I invited them to consider whether law can be used and practiced as a healing art.

I invited them to consider: Into whose hands should the fate of the human species and the whole world be entrusted?

I invited them to consider the extent to which they had and had not taken the law into their own hands in the conduct of their daily lives. I invited them to consider to which laws and in whose hands did they subject themselves if they did not live within their own means. Considering such matters together in Socratic dialog, we widened and deepened our understanding of what makes us and a lot of other stuff tick.

I invited them to consider the meaning of "justice." Is justice that which suits just me, or just you, or just us? Who and what do we include as "us"?

In my introductory class in environmental law, I'd start off with the provocative statement that I hoped that most of the students in the room were not planning to become lawyers. "I think we have too many lawyers already," I'd say. That tended to rivet attention. I'd say, "I think environmental law is far too important to be left in the hands of judges, legislators, lawyers and such."

I greatly appreciated the presence in my classes of those who planned to become scientists of one kind or another, so as to help us all understand how the world really works and to inform policymakers about how best to arrange things in light of that knowledge. You may have heard this aphorism, a maxim of Roman law: "Out of fact comes the law."

The facts—the way the world works—express laws more fundamental than the ones we make up and legislate and adjudicate and seek to steer by. For example, the laws we make up concerning private property do not conform to the way the world really works; when it comes down to it, land can never really be owned as "property." In reality, the land does not belong to us, we belong to the land, and it is our duty to use and care for the land as trustees rather than to assert self-serving rights of ownership of any of it. Ownership of land is a convenient and transient illusion, whereas the consequences of the work we do and fail to do as trustees of the land are real.

Until recently, our knowledge of ecology—the way the world works—has been limited, and our legal notions concerning property rights and duties have been out of step with the way the world really works. Tribal societies whose very existence hinges on their under-standing of the ecological landscape of which they are a part seem to have a better grasp of ecology and property than has been the case with us so-called "moderns."

I invited my students to consider the nature of time, to consider whether and to what extent we are time-travelers. I invited my students to consider if they had the capacity to choose how expansive or constricted they wished the present to be. I invited them to consider whether the living owe duties to the yet unborn members of the species. I would roleplay a person who loudly declaims, "Why should I care about posterity? What has posterity ever done for me?!"

The people of the Iroquois nation conducted themselves in accordance with what they called "the Seventh Generation Principle," which was so well understood and ingrained in their way of being that they did not see any need to call it a law. In accordance with this principle the people took upon themselves the sacred duty to look beyond the limited time of their own lives and to take a long journey of alert consciousness into the future when considering how to be and what to do in the present moment.

The Iroquois people did not travel far in terms of place/space, but they considered it their duty to be time-travelers for the benefit of their descendants. I invited my students to consider whether such a far-seeing principle should be a pillar of environmental law.

Regardless of what work they chose to do, I encouraged my students to become educators in their communities and places of work and to act with compassion and conviction to help further ecological understanding and its teachings. I invited them to examine themselves and their own conduct before criticizing the conduct of others. Because of this "from-the-inside-out" approach, my classes appealed to students interested in the philosophical and spiritual aspects of environmentalism. The student newspaper, *The Daily Nexus*, once described this as "McGinnes brand of spiritual environmentalism."

Over the years I developed and taught ten courses within the Environmental Studies Program, a few of which were cross-listed with Law and Society and the Global Peace and Security programs. Among them were Principles of Environmental Law, Land Use and Planning Law,

International Environmental Law, Environmental Dispute Resolution, Environmental Ethics, Critical Thinking, Thinking about the Future, Ecopsychology and SimCoast (more on that in a moment). It was all a labor of love, and looking back now I'm amazed at how fast it passed by.

I invited my students and fellow professionals also to consider that "feelings are facts." In vintage television's cop show *Dragnet*, Sergeant Joe Friday routinely implored a female victim or witness to set aside her feelings by telling her, "Just give me the facts, ma'am."

The idea that feelings are not facts is pernicious and demeaning and arises out of reductionist thinking, as if reason and emotion were severable in human experience. Yet there's no getting around the fact that we are feeling beings and our feelings govern our actions as often as our reason. Feelings are always with us, and they can't and shouldn't be thrown out of court or the classroom or anywhere else.

By the way, if you walk by the Santa Barbara Courthouse you will see, carved in stone, the words "Reason Is the Life of the Law." By contrast, if you walk by the law school in Berkeley you will see inscribed on an outer wall these words of Justice Oliver Wendell Holmes: "Reason Is Not The Life Of The Law ... It Is Experience."

Which of the two statements do you believe to be more true?

Students who become aware of the environmental devastation that the consumptive economy has brought about in the world can get bogged down in negativity. In my classroom, I tried to provide an antidote to this, to inspire uplifting, positive experiences. I invited students to participate in my practices of centering in gratitude and reverence and to develop their own practices. I invited them to invite their higher selves to express themselves in thought and action.

I used humor, sometimes going to great lengths or rather, great heights, to get a laugh. As described in my book about stilting (*Rise Up: A Stilter's Adventures in Higher Consciousness*), I donned stilts in the classroom to provoke laughter and thought in the classroom. For me being at work doesn't mean I can't play.

What about higher consciousness? Is it an option? My students already thought I was a little odd for talking so much about love and feelings in a law course, so what did I have to lose? I certainly had plenty

Bud Bottoms and Marc McGinnes, 2018. *Photo by Isaac Hernández.*

to gain if I could brighten everyone's day as I invited people to rise into their higher consciousness.

As intelligent animals, we're meant to play, and the new perspectives that come from play can help us at work, too. For people who can't acknowledge the value of play, I have two words of wisdom: Lighten up.

Going through life with a sour, lead-footed disposition isn't a prerequisite for contributing to society. In fact, it holds you back. Laughter is a healing and de-escalating force in a world wounded by divisiveness and fear.

Bud Bottoms, who recently died, was one of my greatest teachers and dearest friends. A leading founder of GOO!, he was a remarkably gifted artist and sculptor, the creator of the magnificent Dolphin Fountain on Cabrillo Boulevard at the entrance to Stearns Wharf. From Bud I've learned the value of mirth in the face of menace and madness, and my memories of his examples of this quality of character never fail to set me to chuckling.

Fun and playfulness were prioritized in a simulation course that I developed with the help of Jim Hurley and David Stone, top notch professionals in their fields in Santa Barbara. SimCoast was an innovative, advanced twenty-week class in which the students engaged in a simulation of the land use permitting process in a typical California county.

Initially, we held the classes in the state-of-the-art Social Sciences Laboratory, where transactions between different negotiating groups could be observed from a central location, so the instructors could watch the dynamics play out.

The students engaged in role play. For most, this was a valuable exercise in coming to grips with the perspectives of other people with different motivations. It was also great acting practice for those who wanted to become trial lawyers or public advocates.

Many trial lawyers are superb actors, because an actor's skills are useful in the exercise of persuasion. I think if I hadn't become a lawyer, I might have become an actor myself. Even though most of my law practice took place in hearing rooms rather than courtrooms, I sometimes resorted to the theatrical methods used by trial lawyers to prove a point. Once, I went up to the speaker's podium before the Board of Supervisors with a big box, dragging it up to a side table and setting it down as if it were really heavy. At the podium, I said, "The proponents of this project have claimed that there are numerous compelling and weighty reasons"—I put my hands on the box as if sensing its weight—"for its approval."

I went on to mention several of the proponents' claims and then announced that we'd examine them for ourselves. Of course, the climax of this performance involved opening the box and revealing its emptiness for all to see. There wasn't a single compelling reason inside.

In experiences like these, I found that laughter, so welcome in the classroom, is often equally prized in the hearing room, the courtroom, and the boardroom, where people are burdened by tensions and responsibilities.

While hard at work I've played on stilts to get my point across, especially to those determined not to listen. Once I appeared before the County Board of Supervisors at a particularly tension-filled hearing to consider a proposal to make changes in the county's environmental review process that I believed would substantially weaken existing protection safeguards.

Marc addressing the County Board of Supervisors, 2005. *Photo courtesy of Marc McGinnes Archives.*

At 8'6" tall on my stilts, I strode to the speaker's podium, eyed the supervisors one by one, cleared my throat and said, "Funny business has its place. But there is no room for engaging in funny business when it comes to the county's environmental protection measures. This proposal is a piece of funny business. I appeal to you as fellow higher-ups to turn it down."

In SimCoast, we had a large cast of characters: three students would act as developers, whose objective was to win approval for a development project based on a real case yet to be decided.

Three students would act as members of the planning staff, who would evaluate the proposed development and make a recommendation for its approval or denial.

Three more students would act as representatives of pro-development community groups such as the Chamber of Commerce or builders' associations.

Three more students would act as representatives of environmental or neighborhood groups.

Finally, three additional students would serve as planning commissioners, to conduct a public hearing at which the others would appear and advocate for their cases. These planning commissioners would then make a decision to approve or deny the project.

From this immersive role-playing approach, students discovered that they couldn't achieve anything by just sitting in their own spaces. They had to talk to people and form alliances. They had to negotiate between themselves and with opposing groups.

The losing side would then file an appeal to a mock board of supervisors seeking to overturn the decision of the student planning commissioners. I'd invite people in the community to play the roles of the supervisors. I liked to cast against type when we did this, because it made for a unique learning experience for both the students and our guests from the community.

For example, I'd ask Andy Caldwell, an aggressively conservative, pro-business lobbyist, to play the role of an ardent environmentalist. And to counter with him I'd ask Linda Krop from the Environmental Defense Center to play the role of an aggressively outspoken pro-growth supervisor. How wonderful it was to see them working together to see who could behave most like the other!

I'd ask other local people involved in the local planning process, including developers and environmental leaders to role-play supervisors of various leanings. My friend Lee Moldaver (the male counterpart of Selma Rubin in his participation in the efforts of just about every environmental and community-interest organization in town) deserves special mention as one of the most knowledgeable and accomplished actors who came from the community to the campus in order to play with us.

The students would run a televised hearing before the mock board of supervisors, and they would make their decision and then stay around to talk with the students. In two subsequent sessions of the class, we'd debrief, getting the students to dissect what happened. If this decision were to be appealed to a higher authority (such as the California Coastal Commission), would there be grounds for appeal and what would the courts be likely to do on a record like this? A key takeaway was always that legal decisions are often influenced by the interactions between personalities, wherein feelings are facts to be taken into careful consideration.

I always took the position in my course that this was a communitarian thing we were doing. It wasn't just within the university's walls, but something we were doing with and for the community. I think it had a real impact on the guests we invited. Andy Caldwell loved the role-playing part of it, and he seemed as sad as I was when the class came to an end when I retired from my regular teaching duties at UCSB.

Lee Moldaver, 2018. *Photo by Nancy Black.*

Each year, I also invited Andy to speak to my courses on environmental dispute resolution, because one of the key ideas in conflict resolution is that understanding doesn't require agreement. The best way to demonstrate this is to try to understand someone with whom you disagree.

So, I'd have Andy come in and he'd do his thing, and he needed no encouragement from me to go over the top in light of what students might have been expecting to hear in class that day. He'd say something to the effect of "You students mess around out here all day, while your parents and the working men and women in the county are doing real work and are being taxed to the hilt so the state can pay for you to play around, do drugs, go to the beach and pretend to be environmentally aware and eco-whatever holier-than-thou. Well, let me tell you a thing or two…"

He'd rail on like this, and most of the students would recoil. Some students tried to break in to argue with him, but he plowed on past the first few who did. Some tried to get up and leave, but I had posted myself by the door and motioned them to remain. Most had tuned him out, and since no one had a device with a screen at this time, I looked at a variety of hostile, bored, disdainful and other facial expressions and sitting positions. The students I prized most were the ones who were listening, simply listening to what he had to say. These were the students who would help me to teach their fellow students that "understanding does not require agreement."

Pete McCloskey once told me that the best reason to go to a really good law school is to be in the company of really good law students (neither Pete nor I were among these) because you were going to get more from them than from the professors. I always appreciated the presence of really good students in my courses, and I was blessed to be in the company of a great many from whom I learned a great deal over the years.

I invited people from the community to contribute their expertise as instructors and guest lecturers for the Environmental Studies Program. Bob Sollen, the journalist from *The Santa Barbara News-Press* who had done sterling work on the oil spill, taught a course each year on Environmental Journalism. David Stone, an exceptionally bright and talented planning specialist, co-taught the SimCoast series with me for several years, and I persuaded Paul Relis, who in addition to his crucial leadership at CEC had served on the California Integrated Waste Management Board, to teach a course each year on Waste Management.

And just as people active in the community stepped in to put a continuing flow of fresh energy into the program, a continuous flow of outstanding young people graduated from the program and emerged into Santa Barbara and across the country to provide fresh energy and environmental expertise.

As the UCSB Environmental Studies Program developed, it was really wonderful to see the quality of the students who flocked to this major, and seeing their success as they put their lessons into practice motivated me to continue teaching there for thirty-three years in a row.

The true mark of distinction earned by the Environmental Studies Program and its graduate counterpart, the Bren School, is this pairing of a high level of scholarship with a track record of community action. Both the Environmental Studies Program and the Bren School have contributed mightily to the marked improvement of the campus's planning and development policies and practices, and today UCSB is widely recognized for its achievements in energy and other resource efficiencies.

I was far from alone as a UCSB faculty member devoting energy to working with environmental groups in the community. Beginning in the early 1970s and to the present, several of them stand out in my eyes, including Barry Schuyler, Cindy Sage, Bob Wilkinson, Paul Wack, Celia Alario, David Cleveland, Greg Mohr, Ed Keller, Mark Schlenz, and David Pellow from the ES Program and Harvey Molotch, Dick Flacks, Richard Appelbaum and John Foran from the Sociology Department.

Among my environmental heroes at UCSB over the many years is Chancellor Henry Yang, whom I used to visit at the beginning of each academic year as one higher-up to another, wearing my stilts. The topic of conversation, of course, was higher education, so I would offer to get him on stilts to achieve it.

Henry is playful. He is also not a man to be pushed around, as an oil giant and its allies tried to do when he first arrived on campus. Mobil Oil wanted to construct a 16 story slant-drilling and extraction platform on a portion of the UCSB campus in order reach nearby offshore undersea deposits, and it had the support of strong political allies. It promised to pay millions of dollars to the university in a steady stream during its operations. On the other hand, there was widespread opposition to the proposal (ridiculously called the "Clearview" project) from the community and on campus.

Henry took a dim view of the proposal and turned down the offer of millions to see things Mobil's way. From that time to the present, Chancellor Yang has strongly supported both the ES Program and the Bren School of Environmental Science and Management, enabling each to become and remain leaders in undergraduate and graduate environmental education in the United States.

In 1980, I wrote my first book, *Principles of Environmental Law*, which was the first of its kind designed for undergraduate teaching. It included not only the overarching principles pertaining to the topic, but also a large number of actual court decisions and provisions of legislative

UCSB Chancellor Yang presenting Outstanding Teaching Award to Marc, 1997.
Photo courtesy of Marc McGinnes Archives.

and administrative law. It was an outstanding piece of work for its time, if I do say so myself. If I had been more entrepreneurial I might have taken it to an established textbook publisher. As it was, I self-published it with a local printing company under the name of Rainbow Bridge Publishing, and I sold it at cost.

I filled orders for the book from a few professors who taught the subject at other universities until all copies were gone, and I gave permission for it to be copied and used thereafter without payment to me. After the originals of the book ran out, my students obtained copies prepared by the campus bookstore. A businessman I am not.

Principles of Environmental Law, 1980.
Photo courtesy of Marc McGinnes Archives.

While teaching, I really enjoyed participating with the workings of campus governance, and so I was an active member on a number of faculty committees, including the campus planning committee and the committee to oversee operations at the Sedgwick Reserve in the Santa Ynez Valley. I was never afraid to rock the boat. That is what boats do, they rock.

I worked for several years on behalf of underpaid and overworked lecturers. Until the policy concerning them was overturned, they were let go after a relatively short term and had to move on, regardless of their teaching abilities and accomplishments. Exceptions to this policy could be made but rarely were. An exception was made for me, thanks to the strong backing of the tenured faculty and deft leadership of program chair Ed Keller, but my commitment to work on behalf of my fellow lecturers did not slacken.

I wrote letters to the deans. I wrote a couple of editorials in the *Daily Nexus*, the campus newspaper. I went to Academic Senate meetings. Eventually we succeeded in forming a union with the vital right to bargain with campus administration over the terms and conditions of lecturers' employment, and we succeeded in working out a new policy that was and remains far more equitable for the lecturer community at UCSB, who shoulder most of the teaching load there so that tenured professors can meet their research and publication obligations.

It was a community-building effort of the kind I am drawn to participate and take a leading part in, wherever and whenever the opportunity arises. I see the whole Earth as a community, and I'm a devoted advocate.

Captain Joel Honey. *Image courtesy of UCSB Library Special Collections.*

We all have the right to the enjoyment of life. So if another is treated unjustly, I want to address that injustice. I care about people being at center stage in their own lives, fully in charge.

In Isla Vista, the student-dominated community adjacent to the university, unrest and notorious police brutality were a too familiar scenario in the late sixties and early seventies. Who were the victims here?

The police deliberately projected an intimidating and violent image and deliberately adopted intimidating and violent policies. Santa Barbara Sheriff's Department Captain Joel Honey was pictured in the newspaper brandishing a medieval-style mace and sword while giving a pep talk to fully armed, helmeted and baton-wielding police, many of whom were brought up from Los Angeles, prepared to do battle.

Anti-Vietnam War feelings were running exceptionally strong among students all across the country in 1970, and it was as if some police commanders, like Honey, meant to bring that war onto the streets of America in order to crush dissent. When young anti-war demonstrators clashed with the police, the cops pursued people into their residences, beating and arresting them in their own homes.

They even beat up a young district attorney, Pat McKinley, who was on the scene in an observer capacity. The Bank of America branch office in Isla Vista and all the money and everything else inside it was burned. Not long after, a student was shot and killed by a police officer while attempting to extinguish a fire that threatened to burn down the trailer set up by the bank to continue doing business.

In the aftermath of the riots, Helen Pedotti and several other prominent civic leaders convened the Santa Barbara Citizens Commission on Civil Disorders. They wanted to investigate the circumstances of the riots, to make findings about what had happened based on testimony and other evidence. I was asked to serve on the Commission and readily agreed.

At age 28, I was the youngest member and had the longest hair. It was most likely for that reason that I was appointed to a subcommittee charged with looking into the motivations, attitudes and actions of the students living in the Isla Vista community.

The first meeting of the subcommittee was held in the home of a prominent retired judge, and the topic of drug use in the student community was raised almost immediately by someone who wondered aloud whether "students hopped-up on marijuana and hash were readily inclined to commit violent acts."

Stifling a laugh, I said, "I have been around a lot of people high on marijuana, and I have never known them to be the least inclined to violence. In my experience, marijuana generally induces peaceful, mellow thoughts and feelings."

The others turned to look carefully at me, and the hostess softly asked, "Mr. McGinnes, I know that my request may be out of line, and you certainly may decline, but I wonder if you would be able to help those of us who have never tried marijuana to experience its effects for ourselves."

"Sure," I said, and pretended to reach inside my jacket for a joint.

Someone blurted, "I don't smoke!"

"How about brownies?" asked another, drawing suspicious looks.

Our subcommittee worked it out, and I provided some excellent bud to the member who volunteered to bake up a batch of brownies for the next meeting. It was mind-expanding for everyone.

I'd had marijuana, but it was a new experience for me to sit in a room full of older people getting a little high and trying to conduct business. We didn't get much done and quickly diverged from the agenda when

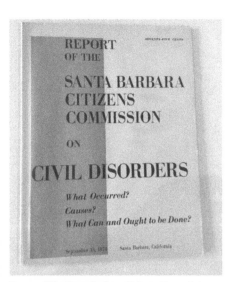

Report of the Santa Barbara Citizens Commission on Civil Disorders. *Photo Courtesy of Marc McGinnes Archives.*

we all got the munchies and ended up emptying our host's refrigerator.

In the end, the basic finding of the commission was that the events in Isla Vista were fundamentally police riots. There had been a few instigators among the students but most of them were peaceful, if angry. By contrast, the police, particularly those who had been brought in from Los Angeles, had mostly gone into the riots in eager anticipation of a fight. There was no suggestion in the commission's report that marijuana had anything at all to do with what took place, but some people wondered what other substances might have gotten Capt. Honey and some of the police with him so aggressively hopped-up.

Irons in the Fire

6

During the early seventies, I continued my activist legal work even as my teaching load increased. Looking back over my calendars from those years, I'm astounded to reflect on the energy I had then to get involved in so many projects, from protecting beach access to providing open spaces that would last for generations, to leading students into the new fields of Environmental Law and Ecopsychology. So many pertinent issues were on the table and I was up for the challenge.

Around that time, a developer proposed to build a high-rise hotel on East Beach. It would have been way out of scale with the existing structures in that area. Under the leadership of Bob Easton and Paul Relis, I worked on behalf of the Citizen's Planning Association and other groups to resist this development, and we successfully averted the Waikiki Beach-ification of Santa Barbara.

Even though the City Council had a pro-growth majority at the time, the writing was on the wall. The constituency was changing quickly in a slow-growth and even no-growth direction. At the same time, Fess Parker, the retired actor known for his years as Davy Crockett on TV, and new to the development business, acquired an interest in the beachfront property we had just protected from development.

A few years later, he proposed to put his own sprawling hotel complex on the beach side of Cabrillo Boulevard. I represented Fred Eissler and Scenic Shoreline Preservation and others to get the hotel to be scaled-back and relocated to the north side of Cabrillo. The City Council approved the relocation, but Fred Eissler and others didn't think the expansive development was scaled back enough to suit the character of the community.

Signatures were gathered to put the issue to a referendum vote to overturn the City Council's decision. We gained enough support to put it on the ballot, but in the end, the voters approved the development. Selma Rubin agreed with the City Council on this matter. It was the only instance I can recall when she and I were on opposite sides of an environmental issue.

Another challenging situation presented itself soon after that. A developer and property owner in Goleta anticipated undertaking a development project which would involve cutting down most of the eucalyptus trees on the property. While eucalyptus trees aren't native to California, they've become an important part of our local ecosystem. Here, Monarch butterflies use eucalyptus trees as a mating stop on their migration journey. The developer wanted to avoid any inconvenience or compromise from following the law that required the delay and scrutiny of an environmental impact report. Hence, the developer decided to cut first and seek forgiveness later.

I got a phone call from a concerned citizen who had heard the sounds of chainsaws cutting trees on the site, and I rushed out there to have a look for myself. I wasn't the only one in a hurry. At that time, my neighbor Frank Frost, a professor at UCSB, and Jim Slater, a lawyer and my friend, were both running for seats on the Board of Supervisors. They dashed to the scene, interrupted the logging and were promptly arrested. This was great publicity for both of them as environmental heroes, and they were subsequently catapulted into office.

We urgently had to stop the cutting, so I did what you do when you require immediate judicial intervention. I filed an application for a temporary restraining order.

A temporary restraining order is a means to get a court order on an emergency basis to stop allegedly unlawful action before a judicial hearing to review the facts of the matter in a more leisurely manner. It requires payment of a sum of money, called a bond, to cover damages to the person accused of wrongdoing in the event that it is subsequently determined that no violation of law had or was about to occur.

Having no client, I filed the case under my own name. This meant that I'd be personally responsible for the bond, which could be substantial. I didn't have time to have the order typed, either, and I printed it by hand, a highly unusual and generally impermissible action.

I called the attorney for the landowner, George Wittenberg, to let him know the request for a temporary restraining order was going to be heard by Judge Arden Jensen. I suggested that he urgently get down to the courthouse to represent his client. In the judge's chambers, I explained to the judge, a straight-laced, reserved man from Solvang, that these trees were being cut down and I showed him a blurry Polaroid photo someone had taken in a hurry. Judge Jensen didn't see that there was anything wrong.

"So? What are we doing here?" he asked.

"That's the point, your honor," echoed George. "What *are* we doing here?"

"Your honor," I said, "This is an attempt to evade the California Environmental Quality Act. This property is owned by a group who intend to submit a development plan."

"But it hasn't been filed yet," objected Wittenberg.

"And this is how they plan to avoid complying with the law by the time they do file one," I continued. "By the time they file there will be no trees, and therefore no roosting for the Monarch butterflies."

This aroused the judge's interest. He sat back, rubbed his temples, leaned forward, adjusted his spectacles and peered at George.

"They're cutting firewood, your honor," said George. I could see by the look on Jensen's face that he didn't quite buy this explanation.

"We urgently need this restraining order, your honor," I said. "They're probably cutting this very minute. If they're not stopped, it'll be too late for the court to intervene at all to enforce the law."

Judge Jensen looked at George and calmly intoned, "If your client is only cutting firewood, they can't be in a hurry."

The judge then turned to me. "Mr. McGinnes, are you prepared to pay the bond now?"

"Well, your honor, as a matter of fact, I am," I said. "Since they're only cutting firewood, I would think that $5 should do."

The judge's dour face cracked into a smile. "That should do," he agreed. George silently fumed.

In the end, with the consent of the property owner, the temporary restraining order became permanent. They decided that the best way to avoid further legal hassle was simply not to cut the trees.

Not long ago, George and I reminisced about this incident, chuckling over our lawyerly antics and Judge Jensen's judicial response. "You ambushed me good on that one," he gamely acknowledged.

I had a similar experience when I served as lawyer for groups that had come together in defense of Hammond's Meadow in Montecito. Before the Spanish arrived, it was the Chumash village of Shalawa. It later was used as an airstrip adjacent to the Hammond family estate. For many years the meadow was also used by the public for coastal access and other recreational purposes. The surf break at Hammond's was popular, so initially surfers, notably the redoubtable Bob Whitney, led the fight to resist development there.

I don't think the Surfrider Foundation existed at that time, but in the intervening years they've done wonderful work, often in partnership with the Environmental Defense Center, to protect the coastline, to the point that it's difficult to imagine what the Central Coast would look like now without the effective advocacy of the surfing community.

A Los Angeles-based developer proposed to construct a large luxury residential complex right in the middle of Hammonds Meadow. Despite our efforts to persuade the Board of Supervisors to deny it, we were unable to do more than to get it scaled back somewhat.

Soon after the board's decision on the project, Californians voted to approve Proposition 20, an initiative that created the California Coastal Commission, which would review construction projects affecting the coastal zone. Voters recognized the value of protecting coastal access and amenities for the public. These assets benefit taxpaying Californians and the many visitors lured here by our state's natural beauty, which is so heavily associated with our beaches.

I had worked with the coalition of people who got Proposition 20 on the ballot. Alan Sieroty and Ellen Stern Harris were notable leaders in this group. Sieroty was a California state senator who sponsored a bill in the state legislature that would have established the Coastal Commission. Unfortunately, at that time there wasn't enough environmental political power in the state senate and assembly for his bill to pass, so Sieroty pivoted to write an initiative that the people of California could vote on directly.

I collected signatures for the petition to get it on the ballot and gave talks to educate locals about this great opportunity to protect our coast. Harris came to Santa Barbara to speak and coordinated with other environmental groups throughout the state. She went on to serve as a member of the very first Coastal Commission.

The vote to create the Coastal Commission came just a week or so after the supervisors had approved the development on Hammond's Meadow, and only minor work had been done on the site in preparation for construction. Once the developer learned of the vote, they rushed to get fully underway as fast as possible.

I believed and they feared that the Act would be interpreted in a way which would require Coastal Commission review and approval, so I filed a lawsuit in Superior Court to get a temporary restraining order to prevent any work at the site until the question of interpretation could be decided by the court.

Alas, this time $5 would hardly be accepted as the required bond. The judge set an amount that was way beyond our means to raise and declined to issue a temporary restraining order to stop any further work at the site.

The developer then raced to do as much grading and other work as possible to establish that it would violate his county-approved development rights to retroactively make his efforts subject to Coastal Commission requirements. The case would turn on a determination of whether or not the rushed work was "substantial" and "in good faith reliance" on its county permit.

Because the case was deemed by the State Attorney General's Office to be of important statewide interest, it joined the case on our behalf. The day after I got this news, I got a call from one of the developer's lawyers, a member of the kind of law firm for which I'd worked in San Francisco, and he asked if he could meet with me in my office.

He came straight to the point. "I suggest that you step very carefully in trying to stop this project. You have no idea of the kind of people you're messing with."

Before he could continue, I smiled and said, "I probably met some of them at the Cabana Hotel up in Palo Alto when I worked there. Kindly give them my regards."

By the time we next appeared in court, a good deal more work had been done. Over my strong objections and those of the representative of the State Attorney General's Office, Judge Westwick ruled the work was substantial and had been done in good faith reliance on its county permit. Thus, the construction could be resumed and completed without a permit from the Coastal Commission.

Despite the court's ruling, the developer further down-sized their plan. They were having financial difficulties behind the scenes, and public pressure from the hostile Montecito community was intense. They still built many homes, but a large part of the meadow was spared, including an area once used as a burial site by the Chumash ancestors who had their village there.

California Indian Legal Services were also involved in the case, providing testimony on the importance of preserving burial sites. When such issues arise, there's often a complication to the usual process, in that you need to keep any drawings representing precise burial sites private. Disclosing the specific location of sites encourages those who would pillage and desecrate them.

The compromise over Hammond's Meadow was a partial victory, but it heralded other, fuller victories to come. It was an example of how citizens and public interest attorneys could wield the new laws to put pressure on pro-growth decision-makers and expose their relationships of cozy comfort with developers. These powerful interests were accustomed to getting their way, no matter what the consequences were to the public good. They were disturbed to see the concerns of their constituencies changing as more residents hopped on the environmental bandwagon, and the new laws were a rude awakening to them.

The practice of public interest environmental law at the level of local land use decision-making requires the exercise of political as well as legal skills. This point was driven home to me during my representation of Tom Hayden and Jane Fonda in connection with their application for a permit to operate a day camp for children on their ranch in the mountains above Santa Barbara.

I helped Tom and Jane to fully comply with all legal requirements, and several environmental organizations voiced support for the approval of the day camp and its environmental education programs. However, Tom and Jane's political enemies—many citing their disagreements over the Vietnam War—exerted strong political pressure on the elected members of the Board of Supervisors. As it turned out, we were successful in persuading a majority of the board not to let such disagreements affect their decision.

Jane Fonda and Marc McGinnes, 1970s.
Photo by Steve Malone, reprinted with permission of The Santa Barbara News-Press.

In later years I became neighbors with Tom and Jane, and I observed first-hand the highly popular educational programs conducted at the ranch. I was delighted to be reunited with Jane recently when the Environmental Defense Center conferred on her its Environmental Hero Award.

Jane Fonda and Marc McGinnes, 2018. *Photo by Isaac Hernández.*

The 1970s was a decade of many important victories for the environmental movement in Santa Barbara and across the country. All kinds of environmental laws were being written by federal, state and local lawmakers, and in Santa Barbara the community was mobilized to see that these laws were no mere paper tigers but laws that had teeth and that citizens could enforce.

The two major groundbreaking laws that were enacted at the beginning of the decade were the National Environmental Quality Act and the California Environmental Quality Act. Both of them are grounded in the common-sense admonition to "Look before you leap." This admonition is made by both laws into a legal requirement, a duty that *must* be fulfilled.

The duty that both laws impose must be carried out by any agency that has authority to approve projects which may have a significant environmental impact. This duty requires these agencies to withhold approval until, and only until, they first conduct a careful review, including public hearings concerning such impacts and their environmental significance, so that these impacts might be avoided or mitigated by appropriate means.

In other words, these laws commanded that decision-makers not go off half-cocked without carefully thinking through the environmental consequences of their decisions. It was, as Pete McCloskey had told me in his call in early 1969, a legal commandment that would require a fundamental change in the ways that government exercised its powers, so long as citizens were vigilant in enforcing the laws.

"Don't be negligent when it comes to making use of the Earth's interconnected and sustaining communities of life. Just say no to actions that damage and impair the capacities of those communities to sustain themselves and us along with them. Act as trustees for the benefit of future generations. Keep the future in mind in making your decisions today!" This and no less the law now commands.

These enactments gave force and effect to Aldo Leopold's "Land Ethic" that he set forth in the remarkable book *A Sand County Almanac* in 1949: "A thing is right when it tends to preserve the integrity, stability, and beauty of the biotic community. It is wrong otherwise."

These enactments command that decision-makers follow the Iroquois path to "fulfill the responsibilities of each generation as trustee for succeeding generations," as declared in the National Environmental Protection Act (NEPA), "in order to fulfill the social and economic requirements of present and future generations."

Bingo! Hadn't we reached the promised land? On paper, you could say that we had. On the land, however, we faced then—and we face now—the forces that drive the short-sighted consumptive economy. We've been in a fight ever since for our lives, the lives of future generations, and for the well-being of the whole Earth.

It is for us to fulfill the promises of these laws, and it seems that we may be at it during all of the time that we are here.

In 1970, I and others brought the Community Environmental Council into being in order to help fulfill those promises.

In 1977, I and others brought the Environmental Defense Center into being to carry this work forward.

As Winston Churchill once said, as the world he loved was teetering on the brink of destruction, "We shall defend our island, whatever the cost may be; we shall fight on the beaches, we shall fight on the landing grounds, we shall fight in the fields and in the streets, we shall fight in the hills; we shall never surrender."

Though powerful forces put the whole world on the brink, we say, "We shall never surrender."

Never.

Defense of the Western Gate

7

By 1977, the Community Environmental Council (CEC) was up and running wonderfully well, and it seemed to me that the moment had come to create the full-time public interest environmental law firm I had envisioned since I first moved to Santa Barbara. The directors of the Santa Barbara Citizens for Environmental Defense chose, at my request, to sponsor what we named the Environmental Defense Center (EDC).

I already had a really good deal on the rent for my law office at 1005 Santa Barbara Street, so I simply took down my "J. MARC McGINNES, Attorney & Counselor At Law" sign above the front door, turned it around, had "Environmental Defense Center" carved on the other side, and made room for the other folks invited to become a part of the EDC team.

Funds for hiring initial EDC staff were obtained from private donors, a couple of foundations and grants provided under the Comprehensive Employment Training Act, a Carter-era program to bolster the economy by providing federal funding for job training.

Marc showing both sides of the sign above the door of the Environmental Defense Center at its original home at 1005 Santa Barbara Street. *Photos by Isaac Hernández.*

The first office of the Environmental Defense Center, 1977.
Photo courtesy of Marc McGinnes Archives.

We were able to attract a team of highly-qualified and committed professionals, including attorneys Michael David Cox, Ed Alston, Tim Eichenberg and Jeff North, as well as land use planning specialist Marc Beyeler. Bob Whitney volunteered to work without salary as director of interns and executive assistant. We also hired Grace Schraft, Grace Moceri and Susan Harnish as staff assistants; Marty Klein as development director; as well as twenty interns from UCSB, Westmont College, Santa Barbara Community College and California Lutheran University.

Michael David had previously represented Coast Watch, a citizens' watchdog group founded by Naomi Schwartz and Ann Marsak for the purpose of enforcing the Coastal Act, and he headed up EDC to carry on the same work. I am pretty sure that no lawyer in the entire state handled more cases before the regional and state Coastal Commission than Michael David did during the critically important early years of these agencies.

Members of the first EDC Board of Directors included Selma Rubin, Supervisor Frank Frost, Bendy White, Cindy Sage, Paul Relis and Phil Marking, and among the attorneys who served on the litigation advisory board were Ken Falstrom, Sydney Minnerley, Frank Sarguis, Bob Goodwin, Ben Bycel and Brian Rapp.

During the first week of EDC's existence, Bob Whitney scheduled a meeting at our offices for the purpose of introducing me to Johnny Flynn and Lee Dixon from the newly-established Santa Barbara Indian Center. Johnny and Lee wanted to know if EDC would represent the Indian Center in its efforts to help prevent the construction of an LNG (liquified natural gas) terminal near Point Conception on land considered by Chumash tribal elders to be sacred land: The Western Gate, a portal that spirits pass through, arriving to presence in the world and departing beyond the world.

Bob Whitney. *Photo courtesy of Alison Whitney Jordan.*

They crisply described the circumstances of the case, and as I listened and questioned them about it, I believed wholeheartedly that EDC should take their case and told them so. I also told them I wished to consult with Santa Barbara Citizens for Environmental Defense directors and members of the litigation committee before a final decision could be made.

A few of those that I consulted were initially skeptical, wondering what such a matter had to do with protecting the environment. One asked if there were any endangered species at the site. To his credit, he considered his question more fully and said, "Oh, I see. The Chumash have been pushed to the brink and now this…." He came on board.

Another asked, "Isn't this really a civil rights case?" I asked if I could tell him the story of what happened to me in Chicago in the summer of 1970. He nodded.

Following the Environmental Rights Day conference at which the Santa Barbara Declaration of Rights was presented, I was asked by Garrett Hardin if I would be willing to serve on the board of directors of the group that he and others had founded which was planning a three-day conference of environmental leaders and activists in Chicago. The name of the group and of the conference were the same: Congress on Optimum

Population and Environment. He said that the group would pay for my flights and lodging. I thanked him for inviting me, and said yes.

During lunch following the opening session of the conference I was approached by one of the delegates, a black woman who was a professor at the University of Chicago. After confirming that I was a member of the board of the sponsoring organization, she asked if I would be willing to attend a session of what she called the Black Caucus, a group of delegates who would be meeting that afternoon. I said yes, and I showed up at the time and place she'd indicated.

There were about 30 people in the room, mostly black, a few Native Americans and whites too. The meeting began with the woman's introduction of me as one of the board members of the sponsoring organization, and one of the group, also a black woman, thanked me for coming and said, "We are very concerned about the purpose and program of this conference. We don't see that a place has been made for our concerns in these proceedings."

She went on to say that she and many other delegates of color were concerned that the environmental movement might deprive the civil rights movement of the participation of white people at the moment they were most needed. "We are concerned that many if not most of the white sisters and brothers that we need to work with us will be drawn away from our concerns and will focus too narrowly on what is 'the environment.'"

"Yes," said another delegate who was white, "I can see it now among my family and friends who, when push comes to shove, will want to work on saving the bald eagle and brook trout and open spaces rather than to help address the terrible condition of the inner cities and other consequences of racial discrimination."

Another delegate, a Native American, said, "I see nothing at all on the program concerning conditions on reservations or the protection of indigenous culture."

Another delegate said, "I don't know about where you come from but in this city the cops and the FBI can murder Freddy Hampton, one of our young leaders, a beautiful young man who was just getting going and who was my friend."

So I told the chairman of the Congress on Optimum Population and Environment board of directors, Richard Lamm (later to become Governor of Colorado), about the caucus session, and we agreed to add a session in which the Black Caucus delegates could make their concerns known and receive responses.

We did so, but few white delegates attended. When the session was over, the woman who had invited me to attend the Black Caucus said to me, "Now you've seen for yourself what my white brother said to you earlier. This movement is going to hurt us if it doesn't address our concerns, and it will hurt the environmental movement too, if it remains indifferent. I pray that you will do what you can to correct this."

When I finished this story, that EDC advisor also agreed that EDC should represent the Santa Barbara Indian Center.

I called Johnny Flynn to set up another meeting with Lee and Bob and me, and this time we were joined by Archie Fire Lame Deer, a medicine man of the Lakota Sioux tribe who was working with the Indian Center on the LNG matter. I told them that EDC would take the case, and Archie invited me to participate in a traditional sweat ceremony to mark the occasion.

On the evening of the ceremony, I was introduced by Johnny to one of the Chumash elders. "Marc, this is Uncle Victor, and he would like to speak with you before we sweat together."

Uncle Victor and I stepped aside and he said to me. "We are grateful for your willingness to help us, but I must first tell you this before we accept your kind offer. I hope that you can see that this is more than a legal matter, and that it's more than a political matter. This will be a spiritual struggle, and before we can accept your offer of help, we would like you to sweat with us, and then we'll see."

We entered the sweat lodge, and as my body suffered in the intense heat, my heart-mind came awake and I humbly prayed, as Archie directed us all, "I give thanks for the opportunity to be and to be a part of the sacred circle of life. I give thanks for the Earth, and for the Air, and for the Water, and for the Fire. I pray for the old and for the young and for the unborn. I pray for the plants and the animals. I pray for those who are in suffering and for those who are in fear that they may be comforted. I pray for all of this, in the name of all of my relations."

When we emerged and had splashed cold water over our bodies, Uncle Victor came over to me and said, "When do you think you can begin?"

When I got home after the sweat that night, I went to bed and lay awake thinking about what Uncle Victor had said, that the Defense of the Western Gate would be a spiritual struggle rather than a legal or political one. Could I transcend the "whiteness" of my experience thus far in my life in order to proceed?

My mind was propelled back to growing up in the Tri-Cities where "non-whites" were effectively blocked from living in Richland or Kennewick, and were confined to a ghetto-like jumble of shacks on the outskirts of Pasco. I remembered the poverty of the reservations to which Native Americans who once lived and fished along the Yakima and Columbia Rivers had been confined. I recalled that the only two black students I ever went to school with were exceptionally-gifted basketball players whose parents were allowed to obtain housing in Richland for that reason.

I remembered driving with my grandfather to the Celilo Falls near The Dalles, Oregon, on the Columbia River. There we watched men clambering over wooden planks secured above the roaring rapids in order to spear and net huge salmon as they leaped high into the air to reach their spawning pools upriver. I was about ten years old, and it took all the courage I could muster just to watch such death-defying feats of these seemingly fearless beings.

I remembered my grandfather nodding encouragement to me as we approached a group of men and boys whose skin glistened with sweat and spray. They seemed to glow with something that seemed stronger even than joy. I remembered the moment when the white-haired man among them turned to us and when he and my grandfather shook hands and began talking.

I visualized myself as a participant in what I was witnessing. Some part of me was clambering over the rocks and the planks among them. I remember the joy of finding that I was one of them and that somehow

Native Americans fishing for salmon, Celilo Falls, Columbia River, Oregon, September 1941. *Photo by Russell Lee, Farm Security Administration, Library of Congress [Public domain], via Wikimedia Commons.*

they were part of me and that we were part of the same… something. I saw the old man whisper to my grandfather and they both turned to look at me. We stood smiling at each other and the old man beckoned to me to step closer. It was an invitation, and I accepted it.

On our way back to Richland, my grandfather told me that his heart went out to the people we had been with there, and I thought that maybe that is what had happened to me: that my heart had gone out to them. Yet it felt like they were now in my heart and so had become a part of me.

As I lay in my bed, some 25 years after I had had that experience at Celilo Falls, I brought my grandfather to life in my mind to ask him for his advice. He said, "Marc, that old man we met and talked with long ago might have seen you in this moment. He might have been Uncle Victor in another form. I think you have been invited once again to take a step forward and to let these people into your heart."

And so I did, and the next morning I set to work.

The plan to build an LNG terminal on the west coast of California originated during the Carter administration when, in response to the "energy crisis" caused by the OPEC embargo, it was decided to fast-track energy production and supply projects within the United States in order to speedily counter the embargo and assure adequate energy supplies to markets within the country.

The first site selected for fast-tracking the LNG terminal was Long Beach, but the proposal drew overwhelming opposition there because of an obvious public safety concern. LNG is an extremely volatile and explosive substance and if it might somehow ignite in the Long Beach harbor it would kill and injure a great many people and do serious damage to the port facilities there.

For that reason the plan was withdrawn, and it was decided to construct the terminal near Point Conception due to its remoteness from people and infrastructure that might be harmed. Special legislation was passed that fixed the Point Conception location and fast-tracked the project to avoid Coastal Commission environmental review and approval requirements. The California Public Utilities Commission (PUC) was given primary review and approval authority over the project, subject to final approval by the Federal Energy Regulatory Commission (FERC) in Washington, DC.

At the time, the PUC was what is known as a "captive regulatory agency," meaning that its decisions more often served what was best for the interests that it was supposed to regulate rather than for interests of the public. While at the Thelen firm, I'd learned that the PUC operated this way, and so I was prepared as a public interest environmental lawyer to take them on with my eyes open and my tools at the ready. It was clear to me that the PUC would make every effort, by hook or by crook, to approve the project as fast as they could.

We immediately inserted ourselves into the grinding gears of the PUC's attempt to approve the Point Conception project in record time. According to a news report of the time, Archie, Uncle Victor, Johnny, Lee and I "burst into" what was intended by the PUC to be a routine hearing in Los Angeles to make way for the project's speedy approval. The members of the PUC and the project proponents, a joint venture between Southern California Gas Co. and Pacific Gas and Electric Co. that went by the name WLNG Associates, were aghast and undone by our intrusion, and there was gavel-pounding and hub-bub galore.

Into this din strode Johnny, to stand at the speaker's podium where he said, "Ladies and gentlemen, we cannot allow you to build this terminal or anything else at Point Conception, because you would be trespassing onto land that is sacred to us. We are here in defense of the Western Gate, and we are here to participate in this and all other of your proceedings and deliberations concerning this project. Our attorney is with us, and I ask him to stand with me here now, to respond to any questions you may have."

There was a deep silence in the room as I walked forward to stand beside Johnny. I said, "I've prepared a petition of the Santa Barbara Indian Center to intervene in these proceedings as a party of record, and I am submitting it to you now."

I walked the few steps to where the chair of the PUC sat and handed the petition to him. His hand was trembling when he took it from me.

That was the formal beginning of the spiritual struggle which went on for the next seven years.

A few days later the first of the highly less-formal aspects of the struggle began to unfold. I was working in the office when I received a call from a woman whom I'd met when she was a Deputy Attorney General in the Environmental Law Enforcement Division. She said, "I've left the Attorney General's office, and I'm now working for a joint venture called WLNG Associates."

This unexpected statement and a lack of impulse control led me to say, only half jokingly: "Sold out, huh? Please tell me you're kidding."

She overlooked my discourteous dig and went on, "A large group of Indians has trespassed on our site out near Point Conception, and they are refusing to leave unless we stop all work there. If they don't leave we're going to have them arrested. I'm calling because one of them says that you are their lawyer."

I responded, "You've reached me at the Environmental Defense Center, the new public interest environmental law firm of which I'm chief counsel. We've intervened in the LNG proceedings on behalf of the Santa Barbara Indian Center. How can I help you?"

"We're very concerned that violence might erupt out there. Would you be available to go out to the site?"

"Right now?"

"Yes, we'll have a helicopter waiting for you at the airport."

I agreed. It's not every day a person of modest means like me gets to go to work in a helicopter.

I rushed out to the Santa Barbara Airport where it was waiting, its blades turning slowly, ready to get into the air. I got fastened into to my seat and we took off. It was a beautiful clear day, and as we passed along the Gaviota coastline, I could see dolphins cavorting in the water below.

As we approached the site, I saw several cars and a large cluster of people milling about and looking up at us. I saw Johnny and Lee and a few others I'd met. There were forty or fifty in the cluster. There were women and children among them. Roughly fifty yards from where they stood was a smaller group of a dozen or so men, and the pilot was in radio contact with one of them as we descended.

The earth was covered in a carpet of winter grasses, except where giant scars from excavation work scored the land. Several bulldozers and trucks stood silent near a huge trench. Briefcase in hand, I climbed out of the helicopter and stepped into one of the more surreal experiences of my life.

Johnny walked to meet me. "We're not going to leave until they promise to stop trenching," he said, loud enough for those who were with him to hear. Various voices from the group rose in agreement.

"Who are the folks over there?" I asked as I saw someone from the smaller group, wearing suit and tie, walking towards us.

It was Al Paisano, the local representative of Southern California Gas Company. Although Al was with the opposition, I knew him from a few prior occasions unrelated to the LNG matter, and I waved a welcoming hand.

When he got to us, he said, "We've notified the sheriff of the situation, and he's prepared to come out and begin arresting people who have no business being here and who refuse to leave."

Before I could reply, Johnny said, "Our business *is* being here, sir."

Setting my briefcase on the ground between us, I said, "I was asked to come out here by one your attorneys, Al, and I've come with a reasonable request. Let's see if we can work out an agreement that will avoid the really bad publicity that will come your way if you choose to arrest any of these people. They have acted peaceably, haven't they?"

Al agreed with a frown, "Yes, but they're all trespassing here!"

Johnny responded, "You're the ones who are trespassing here."

"Let's leave that point for another day," I said. "Johnny, if Al agrees to stop work out here until we can meet tomorrow or later in the week, will you and the others agree to leave for today?"

"I'll ask," Johnny said, and he turned toward the group. Al moved close to me and said, "I don't have the authority to make a decision about it. The project manager is Keith McKinney, and he's standing over there."

"Please bring him over," I asked, "I feel certain that we can work this out without getting the sheriff or the newspapers involved."

Al walked back through the tall grasses toward the other group. Johnny returned and told me, "We'll leave if they stop and not unless."

After about fifteen minutes, we watched Al and another be-suited man make their way towards us. Johnny and I stepped forward to meet them, but Johnny tugged at my arm and sat down as did all the others in the group. "Please sit down too," Johnny whispered, and I bewildered myself in doing so.

When the men were standing in front of us, Johnny said, "Thank you for coming to speak with us. Please sit with us to see if we can come to agreement together."

The image of the expressions on the two men before us is as vivid today as it was then, as they slowly lowered themselves to squatting positions, neither willing to sit unless the other did.

It was a flash of genius on Johnny's part, one of several that I observed throughout the long struggle.

I thought I heard a popping noise from one of his knees as Mr. McKinney introduced himself. "Keith McKinney," he winced. Johnny replied, "My name is Johnny Flynn, and Marc here is our lawyer."

Al said, "Marc, we're here because we're willing to talk about it. But we need an agreement first, from you, that these people won't do this again."

"What are you offering?" Johnny asked, and Mr. McKinney, rising to stand before squatting again, accompanied by several titters from the group, said, "If you leave today, we'll stop for the day and meet with you tomorrow."

"Okay," said Johnny. "We need to get home to eat anyway. Thank you. We can talk tomorrow about where things go from here."

So we all stood, Keith and Al with expressions of both physical and mental relief on their faces.

So, Johnny and the others left in their own cars, not in police cars, having stopped the excavation for that day. I was offered another scenic helicopter ride back, but I chose to ride with Johnny instead.

The next day, the LNG group laid out their case to us. They thought that we should allow them to do the excavation they were doing because they were gathering information about whether the site lay upon an earthquake fault. If it did, the site would be disqualified, and the project would be abandoned. They went on for about fifteen minutes and were about to unroll geological charts, when Johnny said, "What you have to understand is that we can't allow you to continue to desecrate the Western Gate. That's why we came out there yesterday. What you were doing was tearing into the flesh of Mother Earth in a place where you and your machines don't belong."

Mr. McKinney rapped hard on the table, but before he could speak, Johnny asked, "Sir, what would you do if a bunch of people with jackhammers pushed their way into your church and started breaking up the floors? Would you sit quietly by?"

Into the ensuing silence, one of the WLNG group spoke, "I am so-and-so, and I am one of the companies' lawyers and I feel certain that Mr. McGinnes and I could work out a satisfactory compromise."

To that I replied, "I am entirely certain that we could not." Johnny said, "If he tried, we'd fire him," and that brought the meeting to an end.

A short time later, the bulldozers were fired up and work on the trenching excavations resumed. This time they were met with a far greater number of Native Americans, again with women and children among the men, and as before, they brought all work to a stop.

Wary of the bad publicity that would certainly ensue (Johnny and Lee were masters at communicating with the newspapers and other media), WLNG Associates did not summon the sheriff but appealed behind the scenes to the governor to take the matter into hand and, they hoped, get him to behave like Ronald Reagan had when he'd moved aggressively to confront the Berkeley troubles by firing the Chancellor of the UC Berkeley campus and siccing the National Guard on the Free Speech Movement demonstrators.

The governor this time, however, was the young, fresh-faced Jerry Brown, a different sort of man. Like Reagan, Brown had presidential ambitions and was reluctant to risk the awful publicity that would come his way if he came down with a heavy hand. Instead, he quietly opened back-door negotiations with the Chumash Tribal Business Council on the reservation in the Santa Ynez Valley.

As on most Native American reservations, there's a tribal business council whose work it is to do what it can to provide for the economic well-being of tribal members. Securing job opportunities is among the business council's top priorities. The business councils are subjected to immense pressure from "resource extractors" to accept development projects on their tribal lands in exchanges for promises of jobs and money, badly needed to sustain the tribe.

While these negotiations were taking place, the Native Americans who had come to the Point Conception construction site earlier began setting up an encampment nearby, and in a couple of weeks a village had come into being, with more and more supporters arriving. Around a central fire pit and large Army surplus kitchen-tent, there were tee-pees and lean-tos, tents of all sizes, and vehicles of all sorts and sizes, providing sleeping quarters to as many as 150 people on ceremonial occasions and 20 to 30 on most days and nights. Down by the creek a sweat lodge was erected.

These arrangements nearly always turn out to be very bad bargains for the tribe in the long run, as was then perfectly clear by what the Peabody Coal company had done in inveigling the business councils of the Hopi and Navajo nations to allow massive coal mining operations on their sacred lands at and around Black Mesa in Arizona.

Trying to do their best to provide for the Hopi and Navajo people, the business councils there moved ahead, over the objections of their tribal elders, to accept the project.

One of these elders was Thomas Banyacya of the Hopi people, who I met when he came to the Santa Barbara Indian Center at this time, to lend his support for our efforts. Thomas was carrying with him "The Hopi Prophecy," calling upon people everywhere to understand and act in resistance to the onslaughts of the consumptive economy upon the world's sacred communities of life. He said, "My people have been greatly impoverished by the decision to allow the invasion and desecration of Black Mountain, and I bring a warning from them to you and all others to resist spiritual impoverishment and its consequences."

Shortly after Thomas's visit, the encampment near Point Conception was brought to an end when an angry young man from another tribe snuck a gun into our midst and shot another man in the foot over a trivial personal dispute.

The next day, a large contingent of armed sheriff's deputies surrounded the encampment. Johnny and I went to meet their commander, who told us that they'd come to do whatever it took to clear everybody out.

Many of the people in camp were willing to leave immediately, and the commander allowed us to oversee that everyone else would peacefully withdraw in the next few days after dismantling the kitchen tent and the sweat lodge, removing ceremonial objects, and clearing the area of items that had been left behind. After a final sweat lodge ceremony this was accomplished, and the occupation came to a peaceful end.

Before we departed, we were assured by WLNG that individuals or groups less than 10 would be able to come onto the site for "strictly spiritual" (those were the words) purposes and no others.

When Kote Lotah, a young Chumash leader, and a few others attempted to do so a few weeks later, they found that a new chain-link fence and gate had been erected, and guards were posted with instructions to prevent access to the site by any but WLNG personnel.

Kote attached a cable to the back of his pickup truck, attached the other end to the gate, and drove forward, pulling it down. The guards radioed for help and scattered. Sheriff deputies soon arrived and arrested Kote.

On the day that Kote came to court to face charges, he wore a few feathers in his hair and carried with him a beautifully wrought staff, with a large crystal embedded in the mouth of a carved snake. Kote declined to sit in the witness chair on the dais next to the judge, who allowed him to stand for face-to-face questioning about what he had done and why.

Looking down upon Kote from his bench, the judge asked, "Mr. Lotah, I am going to ask you a question, and I suggest that you think carefully before you answer. What if there was something on or about *my* (heavy emphasis) property that you thought for some reason was sacred to you; would you consider yourself at liberty to tear down *my* (even heavier emphasis) gate and interfere with what *I* (emphasis to the third degree) might choose to do concerning it?"

Without hesitation Kote replied, "You're damn right I would, Judge. I have a question for you: "What makes you think that you're above the law?"

The judge sentenced Kote to four days in jail, directed him to pay a hefty fine, and ordered him to make no further attempts to enter the WLNG property.

The money was scraped together to pay the fine, but Kote paid no heed to the order, and he found ways to get there many times thereafter to pray for the land.

Shortly before the occupation came to an end, I received a call from a representative of a Texas-based producer of natural gas, who said that we were right to call the project a boondoggle, and he revealed that there was plenty of natural gas being produced in the United States to meet the nation's reasonably foreseeable energy needs. "America doesn't need to be importing any natural gas from Indonesia," he drawled. "The WLNG thing smells mighty fishy. I think there is something else going on."

He told me that he had long experience working with the Federal Energy Commission and that people there with whom he'd worked in the past were being evasive in responding to his inquiries about the importation of Indonesian LNG to the detriment of domestic natural gas producers. "Yeah," he repeated, "something fishy is going on. You fellows have thrown a monkey-wrench in the works all right, so I hope you can keep at it until we can get to the bottom of things. We sure do appreciate how you've slowed them down."

The "something fishy" about the WLNG project was revealed to me about a week later when a representative of a powerful Washington, DC lobbying firm arranged to meet with me in EDC's office. He explained that his lobbying firm had learned that the overriding reason for the WLNG project was to provide a flow of dollars to prop up the government of the Indonesian strongman Suharto, a strident anti-communist ally of the United States.

Suharto had led the slaughter of an estimated one million communists and suspected sympathizers in seizing control, a campaign that left the Indonesian economy in tatters. The survival of Suharto was seen to be in the "national security interests" of the United States.

With the lobbying firm representative, Johnny and I worked out a plan to spill the beans about this to influential members of Congress and to let it be known that the real reason behind the WLNG project was no longer secret.

Johnny, Lee and EDC intern Laura Cohen and I flew to Washington, DC, where we did that work. Pete McCloskey allowed us to use the phones in his congressional offices to set up meetings and otherwise spread the word about what we now knew. Tom Hayden, who would later become my neighbor after he and Jane Fonda moved up to their Laurel Springs Ranch near Painted Cave, later told me that President Carter had told him that he'd taken heat from a few influential Democrats concerning the Point Conception LNG project, because of its incompatibility with Carter's campaign to promote human rights. Whether or not we had anything to do with it all, the Federal Energy Regulatory Commission soon began backing away from its support of the project.

WLNG completed its trenching excavations and submitted documentation to show that there were no potentially active earthquake faults beneath the project site, but the PUC proceedings went into a lull that prompted the project's proponents to claim that it was "dragging its feet."

The governor had passed word to the PUC that it was attempting to work out an agreement with the Chumash business council to win its approval and support of the project in exchange for a package of economic inducements to substantially improve conditions on the Chumash reservation. Against long odds, Uncle Victor and other tribal elders were able to forestall such an agreement from being made.

When Ronald Reagan gained the White House, it seemed that his administration would attempt to breathe new life into the stalled LNG project. Soon after he took office, Reagan ordered the dismantling and removal of the solar panels from the roof of the White House, and he abruptly

Marc in football gear with gritted teeth. *Photo courtesy of Marc McGinnes Archives.*

extinguished the twenty-two-month-old program that Carter had mandated to prohibit the setting of thermostats in federal buildings above 65 degrees in the winter or below 78 in the summer, a move that was estimated to have saved about 300,000 barrels of fuel daily, while it was in effect. Reagan called it an "excessive regulatory burden."

I was devastated. It was like being hit helmet-to-helmet by a linebacker in a football game. It's not that I didn't expect it, but it really hurt.

One of the next things out of Reagan's mouth was something like, "Okay, we have a National Environmental Protection Act, but now we're going to have a new act that looks at regulatory impacts of NEPA and other environmental protection laws. What is needed now is to get rid of regulations that create brakes on our economic growth and interfere with corporate decision-makers who know best how to achieve it." Some crap like that.

About this time, he also declared that, "when you've seen one redwood tree, you've seen them all."

I wondered which one of the Thelen partners might have penned the words he said, this same man who had indeed enabled the corporate powers they served to come to power in Washington, DC. I gritted my teeth and "girded my loins" for what was coming. I was more determined than ever to keep Reagan from setting foot upon the Western Gate.

In the end, we succeeded in delaying the LNG project long enough that the political and corporate will behind the scheme evaporated, and the Western Gate was saved.

In 1984, the LNG partners put the project on hold, and in 1985 they finally filed a notice of abandonment. They had realized it was over long before then. Against the greatest odds, we had won the spiritual struggle.

This case astounded most political and legal observers, and it proved the mettle of the EDC to take on and defeat even the most powerful corporate interests and political opposition. The record of EDC over the years since then shows many great successes; checking attempts to expand oil drilling operations in the Santa Barbara Channel is but one.

All across the country, however, the anti-environmental forces that were marshalled under the Reagan cabal were on the march and were able to undo far too much of what was accomplished in the 1970s. Defenders of the environment and of environmental rights and responsibilities had to hold on.

To do so would require new and fresh defenders. My classes were brimming with such people, and it was in their direction that I focused most of my efforts for the next twenty years.

Full-Steam Teaching

8

A few years after getting the EDC up and running, I met Betty Williams, a Santa Ynez ranch owner who was becoming deeply involved in the environmental movement. She and others in the area, including Art and Sherry Hibbits, John Weister and Art Walker, wanted to create a plan for the Santa Ynez Valley that would prevent rampant development from taking place at the expense of the agricultural productivity, open spaces and environmentally-sensitive habitats of the area. Betty had attended one of the talks I'd given in the Valley about the EDC's work to assist individual citizens and groups to become effective participants in the community planning process, and we talked briefly afterwards.

Betty Williams. *Photo courtesy of Seyburn Zorthian.*

Betty had a law degree, but had chosen not to practice law. She said that she'd like to learn more about the EDC, and I offered to meet with her in the future. A week later, I opened a letter from her that contained a four-figure check and an invitation to call her to arrange for me to come to a meeting of a planning group that would be held at her home at Buttonwood Farm.

When I handed her check to Selma, who was the EDC treasurer at that time, Selma told me that among Betty's other work was careful and generous philanthropy such as that which Kit Tremaine had long provided to the Santa Barbara community. I learned that Betty and Kit were cousins and members of a family of considerable wealth. Selma expressed excitement that I had met Betty and would have an opportunity get to know and work with her. Selma knew everybody.

I telephoned Betty to thank her for her generous gift and to say that I would be pleased to talk with the Valley planning group. We set the date and time for the meeting, and she told me that the chairperson of the planning group was Seyburn Zorthian.

When the day of the meeting arrived, I drove over San Marcos Pass, past Lake Cachuma and into the Valley and to Betty's home. In my head, I was thinking what I planned to discuss with Mr. Zorthian, Betty and the other members of the planning group. I was looking forward to seeing Betty again and I wondered if Mr. Zorthian were a planning professional or not. Seyburn Zorthian. An exotic name. Armenian, I supposed.

I arrived and was getting out of my car, when I looked up to see walking toward me one of the most beautiful women I have ever seen. She smiled warmly and reached out to shake my hand. "Welcome, my name is Seyburn Zorthian. Not everyone is here yet, but come on…"

I didn't follow the rest of what she said, as my mind was in full boggle mode at news that Mr. Zorthian was actually Ms.

"Ms. Zorthian," I stammered, "I'm pleased to meet you."

"Please call me Seyburn. Betty is my mom. May I call you Marc?"

And by those names we have called each other for the past forty years or so. Sometimes "Dear" and "Honey" too.

Marc and Seyburn Zorthian. *Photo courtesy of Marc McGinnes Archives.*

At that point, I'd been single for about seven years and had begun to feel the desire to make another attempt at marriage and parenting. I already had a few names in mind for a future child. My heart fluttered at the thought that the name of its mother might be the erstwhile "Mr. Zorthian."

I was not certain that I was ready to marry again. My beloved son Skye was now thirteen and an absolute joy in my life. I had agonized at times over being "only" his part-time parent. His mother Kathy was a wonderful co-parent, and our lives were closely and lovingly aligned.

"Once married and divorced, twice shy to marry again," my mother used to say when I was growing up, and she was now happily married for the third time.

She also used to say, "Nothing ventured, nothing gained."

With Betty's warm blessing, Seyburn and I married in 1982 and our son Zach was born the following year. I was now a house-husband and full-time teacher. I now felt ready to leave my law practice entirely, to dedicate myself to my family and to full-time teaching.

Marc, clean-shaven, 1983. *Photo courtesy of Marc McGinnes Archives.*

Throughout this time, I was in high gear, in a state of bristling creativity and boundless energy. After I handed the reins of the Environmental Defense Center into the wonderfully capable hands of others, I threw myself into my teaching at UCSB and occasionally at the Santa Barbara College of Law, and I also began to develop my thinking and writing on the concept that law can be used and practiced as a healing art.

I was moved to write an essay called "Law As A Healing Art", or "LawHa" for short. It fueled a lot of new activity for me and became the basis for a number of speaking engagements at conferences for lawyers and peacemakers around the country. It was time to teach ecologically about the law in order to overcome the idea that "conflict is a contest" and a zero-sum win-or-lose game.

I was one of the founders of the Peaceful Resolutions Institute, along with Gail Rappaport, John Jostes and others. Our purpose was to induce lawyers and others to approach and seek to resolve conflict collaboratively rather than competitively. At this time I also helped to create, along with Brian Burke, Nancy Madsen and like-hearted others, a new committee of the County Bar Association to carry forward the LawHa principles and practices.

The Peaceful Resolutions Institute sign. *Photo by Isaac Hernández.*

What a whirlwind time it was! By one name or another the transformational LawHa principles could be seen to be taking hold in the Santa Barbara community and all across the country. It was a shift in context. "Let's make community. Let's not make war among ourselves and with others. There is a peaceful path if we choose to take it."

I was guided by words that came to me one day on the beach after a clarifying swim in the sea:

"Yes, I am I, and you are you,

And we are several among the many.

And yet I am you,

And you are me, and we are one.

All One."

I was grateful to be a part of the development of the Environmental Studies Program at UCSB.

Its innovative interdisciplinary approach enabled us to consider environmental problems from an appropriately inclusive "both/and" perspective, rather than a confining "either/or" one. The vantages of the physical and natural sciences, as well as those of the social sciences and humanities, were considered in a holistic manner, and in time our example led to the widespread adoption of interdisciplinary collaboration between departments all across the campus.

I was afforded wide leeway in developing and teaching my courses as I saw fit. There's that old saying, "If you can't do, then teach." That's just not true.

If you can teach, there's little that you can't do if you put your heart into it.

My favorite course was one I created to explore the topic of Ecopsychology. I was turned onto this idea by Mike Kresky and Warren Brush, then working together with the Wilderness Youth Project. The purpose of Wilderness Youth Project was to address the serious condition of "nature deficit disorder" that afflicts human beings when we don't experience ourselves as part of nature and nature as a part of us.

The following facts are generally acknowledged as true:

1. Human beings like us emerged some 200,000 years ago on the planet and relied on their abilities to mesh into the workings of the environments in which they lived in order to survive and sustain themselves. Had they not done so, we would not be here now.

2. Civilization as we know it came into being around 60,000 years ago at various places on the planet, marking the beginning of human efforts through agriculture and husbandry to gain some measure of control over the environments upon which they were dependent.

3. The "industrial revolution" began some 200 years ago, in the relative blink of an eye, as in 0.1% of time since our emergence here and in 0.3% of the time since our first civilizations came into being. In that brief fraction of time in the history of our species, the relation between people and the rest of the communities of life on the planet has been drastically altered to the profound detriment of both.

Efforts to control and dominate nature have done great damage.

To step into the full potential of our humanity would be to exercise self-control and act with empathy and compassion towards each other and other beings, to think and act as Earthlings with appropriate gratitude and humility and expansive empathy in relations with each other and with the Earth itself.

Our most fundamental evolutionary task as a species is to come to our senses about who it is we think we are in the midst of everything else in the world, in God's creation, as some would say.

Being fully human is to understand that all of life and the Earth itself are holy.

No fully human person could possibly see the Earth and any of the communities of life as merely material "natural resources" to be capitalized upon. No fully human person could act as if economic profit were both the top and bottom line.

Coming to reverence is our evolutionary task right now.

Technology cannot perform this task for us, but it can be used, if wisely, to help us come to a higher Whole Earth consciousness at this momentous—even epic—time on our long journey to who and where we are.

It is time to wake up to the opportunity to become fully human beings and to emphatically—even lovingly—embrace rather than exploit the Earth.

This is not the time to let ourselves and the Earth go to hell.

Speaking of hell, I confess I've never believed in such a place in the afterlife stories that are told in some religious circles. I suppose that the reason for this is the many hours I spent as a boy leafing through the images in the book *The Divine Comedy of Dante Alighieri* that features engravings by Gustave Doré depicting the hideous things going on in the supposed underworld. What I concluded was that Doré had a magnificent imagination concerning a place that neither he nor anyone else had seen or provided a first-hand account for.

But from my own experience I know that we are capable of making things hellish for ourselves on the Earth, and one way we can do this is to put too much hope in the claim that technology can save us from the consequences of continuing willy-nilly along the path of the consumptive economy. For, example the hope that technology will enable us to make Mars our next home.

During the week of Earth Day in 1991, *LIFE* came out with as issue on the cover of which was not Earth, but Mars; and its bold font captions read: "Our Next Home: Mars" and "Bringing A Dead World to Life."

Later in 1991, I read somewhere the words of an official at the National Aviation and Space Administration (NASA) who said, "I think it foolish to put all of our eggs in one basket. It would be wise to look for a place other than Earth. Maybe Earth2. A place where this species could make a new home. Let's learn how to terraform Mars."

In response to those words, I convened a gathering of students on campus, to which members of the community were invited. The event was billed as "A Conversation with Dr. Marslove, Expert on Making Mars Our Next Home." I began by introducing myself as Dr. Marslove, a colleague of Dr. Strangelove, and without more, I said the exact words that the NASA scientist had spoken. I then took a very long pause to adjust the too-small lab jacket I had found for the occasion, to adjust the necktie I wore under it, to clean my glasses, to take a series of sips of water from the glass on the lectern. Finally, I invited comments and questions from the audience.

The first person from the audience to comment was a student who asked, "Are you really a scientist, sir, or are you a science-fictionist?"

I thought it was a fine beginning, and we all took it from there for the next hour or so.

"Earth2? Next in a whole series?"

"Our species? Any others?"

"How many of us? How many will each rocket hold?"

"Terraform Mars? Will there be redwood forests?"

"Any good surf spots in mind, Doctor?"

"How many dollars will this all cost?"

"What about the 2nd Amendment? Guns will be allowed, right?"

And so forth. And so on.

And such nonsense goes on right up until now, when this year we saw ads on television in primetime where *National Geographic* pushed the line that "Mars is our destiny" and that "Our mission is to make Mars our next home."

And creepier still, a recent cover of the National Geographic, pictured what the "Next Human" will look like who will presumably be living on Mars or Earth2 after a shattered Earth is left behind.

Does the consumptive economy mean to try to fit into our bodies a bunch of new "ingredients" so that we can go on being its servants if we wish to survive?! It quite obviously means to do just that if Earthlings let them have their way.

Marc with reading material, including E.F. Schumacher's *Small is Beautiful*, *National Geographic* featuring "The Next Human" and *LIFE* magazine with Mars on the cover as "Our Next Home". *Photo by Isaac Hernández.*

Along the way to becoming who I am today, I was blessed to come across a book, *The Voice of the Earth: An Exploration of Ecopsychology*, written by Theodore Roszak.

"Does the Earth have a voice?" I wondered, as I began to read and reflect. What I discovered was the perspective that it was the Earth's voice that I'd heard when I reverently observed it for the first time from outer space. It was the Earth's voice which called me to listen and seek to understand, enabling me to see that my calling in this life is to be a voice for the Earth and to pass along its messages to others. The Earth called me to do what I could to muster other voices to speak and act for the Earth.

I did what I could to help bring into being the environmental move-ment, to give voice for the Earth, and to inspire others to listen to and act upon its messages to our species. Hearing such messages, that he seems to have received throughout his life, the great David Brower declared, "It is healing time on Earth."

David Brower. *Photo courtesy of University of California at Berkeley, David Brower Center.*

This I have come to know for certain: we don't live inside our bodies; our bodies live inside of us. Our selves are not confined within our skin. Our selves extend to all we apprehend around us. That is the Earth's essential message for us, and an essence of what the field of ecopsychology is all about.

Michael Cohen was the person I came to know who had developed an innovative and effective online curriculum to teach the principles and practices of what he called "Applied Ecopsychology". In it, he asserts that we have 52 senses, not just six, and that we can use them to become deeply re-connected to nature in the midst of the hub-bub and confusion of numbing consumptive culture that makes zombies out of citizens. My students and I used his book, *Reconnecting with Nature*, to learn how to heal the nature-deficit disorders in our lives.

Ecopsychology teaches that we—each one of us—are coextensive with everything that we can see and sense in other ways. Just think what it could mean to recognize and act upon a deep sense of belonging. Just think what that could do to free us from the insane notion that nature is just a supply of "natural resources" that belong to us, to be used up to satisfy our demands.

Try this: choose a place somewhere outdoors away from the din and sit quietly there, once or twice a day for fifteen minutes or so, observing very closely what is going on. Keep doing so, day after day, as if you are engaged in a bit of serious empirical research to see what happens there and what is happening with you. Keep at it, as an experiment which could change your perception of who and where you are. Take notes if you like, to make a record of your discoveries.

My students and I discovered that when we really made ourselves part of a place, that place really became a part of ourselves.

You might begin to sense that all of life is interconnected in more than just a material way, that we are a part of a sacred circle of being, and that we can be grateful to be able to do what we can to assure that this circle remains unbroken.

In the late 1990s, I began to consider taking a break from my teaching and duties at UCSB to live and teach overseas for awhile. In 1999, I applied for a teaching opportunity in Spain but wasn't accepted, but my keen disappointment turned to joy when I received a phone call just a few days later.

On the other end of the line was the academic dean from the Semester at Sea program, who invited me to join the faculty on the around-the-world voyage set to depart in early January, 2000. Upon learning of

Seyburn's distinguished work as an artist, he invited her to join the faculty, too. Zach would also be a member of the shipboard community, and he would complete his high school junior year amidst the undergraduate students.

On January 11, 2000, Seyburn, Zach and I departed from Jacksonville, Florida aboard the SS Universe Explorer and headed for Havana, Cuba, the first port of call of the 111-day voyage. Other ports would include Salvador, Brazil; Cape Town, South Africa; Mombasa, Kenya; Chennai, India; Penang, Malaysia; Ho Chi Minh City, Vietnam; Hong Kong, China; and Kyoto, Japan.

It was a unique and challenging teaching and learning environment and there were a great many wonderfully exciting and deeply moving moments along the way. On the whole, my favorite days were those on the open sea with no land in sight, the vast sky spread above and all around. I sang and danced my love songs to the planet, sometimes weeping with the joy at the splendor of it all.

I renewed my love vows to the Earth one clear celestial night when I saw the Southern Cross for the first time.

A couple of my students on the voyage were among the brightest and best I have had in my long teaching career. When it was learned early on that the ship's garbage was being dumped at night into the sea, several of my students created and led a group—the "Trash Talkers"—that investigated the ship's waste management and dumping practices. They went further and researched the laws and best environmental practices applicable to them and attempted to convene a meeting to inform the shipboard community of their findings and recommendations for better environmental practices on future voyages.

In the eyes of the ship's captain, this initiative was an affront to his supreme authority in all matters aboard the vessel. While he was an affable fellow when not aroused, he was furious with me and the students for acting as if we were citizens, taking the law into our own hands, as if we were members of a democracy. He ordered the students to desist from their efforts, and when the students objected, the captain dropped the M-word: "If you proceed against my order, you will be in mutiny aboard this vessel."

What a splendid teaching and learning moment! It was a perfect opportunity for the students and the entire shipboard community to consider the idea of mutiny in the context of the efforts of well-informed people aboard the ship, or anywhere else, to insist that best environmental protection practices be developed and applied.

One of the students suggested changing the name of the group to "Environmental Mutineers." It was food for thought and for thinking twice before trumpeting it about, given that the captain was on the edge of blind fury.

"Is environmentalism somehow a 'mutiny' in challenging the rape of the natural world?" I asked my students to think and discuss and write about this throughout the remainder of the voyage. It's a question that I invite you as well to carefully consider.

As for myself, I am grateful to act as a "mutineer" in the face of any authority which condones environmental indifference and abuse.

In my teaching, I encouraged my students to both "Question Authority" and to "Question Those Who Question Authority."

"Question authority." *Photo courtesy of Marc McGinnes Archives.*

As the ship moved on, I became increasingly discouraged by witnessing nearly everywhere (except, most notably, in Cuba and Vietnam) the apparent triumph of soulless materialism. I was sickened by the stark vision of ongoing great harm to the Earth.

I returned to Santa Barbara in a troubled state of mind and spiritual unease. The state deepened precipitously when the United States Supreme Court defied long-established precedent to intervene in the presidential election and elevate George W. Bush and his gang into power.

I'd argued forcefully with Ralph Nader during the campaign to withdraw his candidacy to make room for Al Gore, and to stop once and for all from identifying himself as a crusader for so-called "consumer rights." I told him that I thought that it was time to get rid of the idea that citizens are consumers first. I thought if he said so, it would be widely noted and commented upon. He flatly declined. In any event, his refusal to drop out of the race in favor of Gore, a dedicated proponent of environmental rights and responsibilities, was a key factor in the final results.

I despaired as I witnessed the actions of the likes of Bush, Cheney, Rumsfeld, Rice, Wolfowitz and Rove before and after the attack that brought down the Twin Towers in New York City on September 11, 2001.

Despite the fact that the attack was carried out by an al-Qaeda team of mostly Saudi members whose leader, Osama bin Laden, was the privileged son of a father with close ties to the Saudi rulers, millions of Americans and I were horrified by the efforts of the Bush cabal to stir up war against Iraq. We were further horrified when Saudi officials were allowed to bolt the country before they could be questioned about Saudi ties to the team who had performed this act of war against the United States.

As the war-drums from the Bush administration beat louder and louder, I jumped at the chance to go to Iraq as part of a delegation of professors and peace-activists to meet with Iraqi professors and government officials.

In defiance of travel restrictions, we flew to Iraq via Jordan and met with our Iraqi colleagues in various places in Baghdad and nearby. In the midst of the carefully planned meetings, I took the opportunity to move around on foot through the crowded streets, among people going about their business. One day, I played hooky from a luncheon event and wandered onto a bridge to take photographs of the city and fishermen at work from the skiffs on the Tigris River.

I'd failed to see the sign that prohibited taking pictures from the bridge. As I was clicking away, I heard a man shout and looked to see a soldier with a rifle on his shoulder striding quickly toward me, his expression an unforgettable combination of astonishment, anger, and fear. He unshouldered his weapon as he approached and leveled it at me.

He stopped and motioned for me to step forward and hand my camera over to him, which I promptly did. He barked a command at me and motioned me to start walking in front of him with my hands in the air to the end of the bridge where I'd entered. There he showed me the sign and again shouted at me. Clearly, I was under arrest.

UCSB lecturer detained by police while in Baghdad

Man speaks with Iraqis on war

By LEAH ETLING
NEWS-PRESS STAFF WRITER

Less than a week ago, Iraqi police in Baghdad detained Santa Barbara's Marc McGinnes for taking pictures of a bridge over the Tigris River.

He had good reason to be apprehensive, given Saddam Hussein's animosity toward Americans and the looming possibility of war. The officers escorted Mr. McGinnes on a 2-mile walk to two different police stations, confiscated his film and repeatedly questioned his identity.

But instead of worrying about being locked up, the environmental attorney and UCSB lecturer took the three-hour interrogation by police as a chance to learn more about the average Iraqi's view of the U.S. That was his goal during the four days he spent in Iraq with 35 other educators from U.S. universities, meeting with professors

RAFAEL MALDONADO / NEWS-PRESS
Marc McGinnes saw his three-hour interrogation as a chance to learn more about Iraqis' views of the U.S.

own travel expenses. All signed a statement declaring their opposition to war in Iraq before being invited.

Mr. McGinnes, one of three California professors who made the trip,

News of Marc's arrest in Baghdad, January 23, 2003. *Santa Barbara News-Press Archives, used with permission.*

Over the next three hours, I was detained and questioned by two different sets of English-speaking interrogators: Why was I in Baghdad? Why had I gone out into the city by myself? And why had I been taking pictures from the bridge?

It was obvious that they suspected me of spying, and it was clear that if I were a spy, I'd have been in danger of harsh treatment at their hands.

I figured that my absence from the group had been noticed by now, that calls were being made, and that one of our host officials would come and get me out of the mess I had created for myself, our delegation and our hosts. I was more embarrassed at myself than afraid for my safety.

By the time a representative of the host delegation arrived to collect me, the interrogators and I were talking easily, and I was just about to answer the question one of them put to me. Did I think that my country would attack theirs?

I was hustled away in a waiting car with its engine running before I could reply other than to say—and to mean with all my heart—the Arabic phrase that I had been told meant, "May peace be with you and with us all."

Two days later, I was asked by the wife of the Chancellor of the University of Baghdad the same question. "Is war coming?"

She was a formidable presence. She commanded to know what I truly believed, and I said to her, as she held my hands in hers, "I fear that it is, although all of those with me and most people in our country are opposed to those who want it. I urge you to do whatever you can to find safety, to leave Baghdad if you possibly can."

She began to softly cry and so did I: she, my Iraqi mother; me, her American son, weeping together at the prospect of the coming terror.

When I returned to Santa Barbara, I wrote articles and gave talks about the plight of the people of Iraq, "people just like us," and spoke at rallies in the community against going to war, but the devastating attack soon took place, and I again wept for my Iraqi mother and my brothers and sisters there and in my own country.

From all that I had read and heard and considered carefully as the Bush cabal pushed its bogus "preventive war" arguments, it was clear to me that the real motives behind the planned aggression had to do with the control of the oil and water resources of the region.

Dave Brower often said, "There can be no peace on Earth until we learn to make peace with the Earth."

I subsequently learned that many of the Iraqi men and women I had met in Baghdad had been killed, and I slid headlong into a depression that got deeper and deeper over the following weeks, months and years. The prospects of peace on and with the Earth seemed to be diminishing to a point of no return.

Losing Heart

9

I have always been strong, healthy and physically active. As a young man, I played hard at baseball, football and rugby. As an adult, I have kayaked fearlessly and stilted avidly. In 2002, I began to experience sleepless nights and shortness of breath. Stress with a capital S was wracking my mind and my body. My blood pressure was shooting upwards at a rate which led my doctor to refer me to a cardiologist for a check-up. I felt as if I were beginning to burn out.

I was wired up and asked to step onto a treadmill whose speed was increased from a walking to a running pace. The last thing I remember before I came awake on the floor, the stench of ammonia salts burning in my nose, was what looked like an atomic mushroom cloud. "Did I have a heart attack?" I asked, but the doctor didn't say.

Eventually I was released to return home and told to rest quietly for the next several days. I wondered if this "incident" might mean that I would have to rest quietly for the rest of my life. I resolved to fight for my life. It was not time for me to just drop over dead. Not yet.

I learned that my heart was now beset by a condition called atrial fibrillation ("afib") or irregular heartbeat, which would require careful attention for the rest of my life. Tests revealed that I had also developed a condition called sleep apnea, which had been interfering with my ability to breathe easily during sleep. So, I was fitted for a CPAP device and began taking medications that my body now required and does to this day.

These events led me to decide to retire from my full-time teaching and administrative responsibilities at UCSB, and I set out to find others to pick up those reins. I am grateful to report that I succeeded in doing so, and the courses that I had started in environmental law and ecopsychology continue to this day in the wonderfully capable hands of Linda Krop and Lori Pye, respectively.

My colleagues at the university generously provided a retirement event at which we shared our love of our work and each other, and the faculty of the Environmental Studies Program did me the honor of creating an annual scholarship and award in my name. A record of this memorable event, containing appreciations from students and some of their favorite "Marc-isms," can be found on the Program's website today. http://www.es.ucsb.edu/people/j-marc-mcginnes

These dear folks also sent me off with a pair of kayaks in which I've paddled coastal waters and in rivers and lakes from Washington State down to Baja California, recalling their kindness all along the way.

When I officially retired from my position I still deeply wanted to continue my studentship, my learning, because that's what, essentially, I loved about teaching. It was a continuous learning experience. I soon developed a few courses for adult students enrolled in UCSB's Continuing Education Program and taught there from about 2005 through 2008.

With students closer to my age, I readily shared my personal struggle to find hope in the midst of despair, and I learned that they were eager to share with me their own stories about keeping on while feeling down. My peers can take this, I realized, and I need help, I need the support of others.

As we considered the topic of "balancing property rights and responsibilities," for example, we created the space to share our deepest wisdom about the future for our children and grandchildren and people everywhere in the face of the vivid evidence that continued "business as usual" practices seemed to be robbing them of a sustainable future of well-being with the Earth. In this lively circle we older folks could talk about what we could, at this point in our lives, do better.

This kind of teaching helped me build the muscles I needed to lift myself out of deadening despair. What I learned was that I was resisting what I should be feeling more fully. I realized I can still breathe even though I am in despair; that I still have the heart and my tools to pick myself up and to carry on with my work.

During this period of recovery and re-emergence, I spent a great amount of time in Baja California, where my family has a modest beach house overlooking the Pacific, south of Rosarito Beach. It offered a soothing change of pace in which to find my footing for the rest of my journey.

Marc standing to paddle his flat-bottom canoe in pre-paddleboard days. *Photo courtesy of Marc McGinnes Archives.*

When I wasn't immersed in the water, I enjoyed walking for hours along the beaches and in and atop the nearby canyons and mesas. I formed a close friendship with the caretaker of the place, his family and many of his friends. I felt myself to be a member of the Mexican communities of La Misión and Santa Anita on the banks of the Guadalupe River near its placid, bird-filled opening to the oncoming breakers from across the wide Pacific Ocean.

One day, I was walking along the beach, stretching in preparation for my morning swim, and a song began to sing in me. It came at first as a kind of murmuring melody and then emerged from me, and I was astonished to hear my voice singing out loud, "Thank you, thank you, thank you," over and over again. It was a simple hymn of gratitude, and as I became accustomed to being sung by it, I abandoned myself to it.

My voice grew louder and more confident and I was filled with reverence and joy. This is the moment when I was shown (by what? from where?) the power of centering in gratitude, beyond all hope.

The song came to me as a blessing. I felt gratitude for simply being alive, for the light and dark, the good and the bad. Gratitude begets blessings. This song gave me the lightness of being and the grace I needed to carry on my work in the fulfillment of my purpose for this lifetime. I was awestruck to the marrow of my bones, or as one of my colleagues from Scotland would say, "gob-smacked to the max."

Being sung by what I came to call *The Thank You Song* I felt a lot like that spellbinding night when I felt the glow of the Earthrise projection lift me into another dimension. The moment grabbed me and held me ever so gently. When that happened, I had a knowing that was beyond words, filled with clarity and absolutely no doubt. I was firmly at my center and powerfully on my path again. The Santa Barbara High School Madrigals sang it gracefully. (Search for "SBHS Madrigals Thank You Song" on YouTube to hear it).

As if to put an exclamation point to this affirmation, a few weeks later on the same beach as I stood singing this hymn of gratitude, "Thank you, thank you, thank you..." my whole body began to move and to "sing" yoga-like movements expressing an inner song that had not come from my mind. Thus came to me what I call "Body Songs of Reverence."

I've taught both the gratitude and reverence songs to hundreds and hundreds of people since they came to me. I feel it's an opening for others to come to the center of their being and to enable them to do what they see fit in the world. It's a blessing beyond measure to see how it helps others to become more fully present.

To be fully present in the moment is what is most needed, if we wish to do what we can to be effective voices for the Earth.

In late 2006, I traveled alone to New Zealand and Australia where I moved along the roadways in a rented camper-van and by bus, with a couple of flights in between. While in Wellington, I was hospitalized briefly by another scary incident with my heart that was originally thought to be a heart attack. In my heart-mind I had made my farewells, and I wondered if my spirit would pass through the Western Gate or somewhere closer by. Perhaps at a sacred place of the Maori, or at the soaring rock domes of Uluru-Kata Tjuta held sacred by the aboriginal people of Australia.

I was not afraid of dying any place along my journey "down under," and I'm not afraid of dying anywhere else. As if to confirm my courage about it, I got into bungee cords and jumped into space from a bridge above a gently curving river far down below. Heck, I was a mere 64 years old at the time! I am still bolstered by the thrill of it, some 13 years later. I would happily do it again!

When I got to Oz (local lingo for Australia), I went first to Adelaide, the boyhood home of one of my Santa Barbara friends, Mike Brown. I then took what was called "The Wayward Bus" north to stay in an underground hostel in an opal mine at Coober Pedy, then on to Uluru-Kata Tjuta. I could feel the presence of that place from fifty or so miles away, and when my young wayfaring companions and I arrived, my heart-mind-body was set to singing its songs. I surrendered myself to the heartbeat of the world that I sensed with all my being there. The heartbeat was strong and from time to time it seemed to skip a beat, just like mine, and then go on.

I went on to visit my friends John and Lynne Boland in Byron Bay and former SBCED director Norm Sanders and his partner Sue Arnold nearby. Norm had moved from Santa Barbara to Tasmania in the 1970s and he'd had a remarkable career as an environmental activist and elected leader there, including service for many years as a member of the Senate of the Australian legislature.

Sue was and is today a well-known journalist and environmental leader there. Norm described himself as a "cranky old bastard," to which Sue nodded her amused agreement, but in them, and in John and Lynne, I felt linked as fellow citizens of the world, a feeling that did my heart a whole lot of good.

When I got back to Santa Barbara I felt buoyed up and ready to resume my work, and for the next five years I fought a losing battle to preserve the beauty of a bridge and to confront the idea that to prevent even one person from making a suicidal leap from it was worth practically any price at all.

At the entrance to the Cold Spring Arch Bridge near the summit of the San Marcos Pass roadway through the Santa Ynez Mountains above the Santa Barbara-Goleta coastal plain is a plaque which proclaimed it to be "The Most Beautiful Single Arch Bridge." Passing over it, motorists and cyclists get an airborne rush in the midst of breathtaking views. No pedestrian walkways were constructed along the roadway, and there were no tall barriers constructed on the sides of the bridge. It took some vanity on the part of the builders to put that plaque on the bridge, but the claim was obviously borne out.

In 2007, the County Sheriff and others asked the State Transportation officials (Caltrans) to construct fencing along the sides of the bridge in order to prevent people from making suicidal leaps into the canyon below. Between 2007 and 2012, I worked with many others in the community to prevent such an action without a thorough-going review by transportation authorities of the environmental impacts involved and of the assertion that such fences were the sole best life-saving, suicide-prevention strategy to pursue.

I emphasize "life-saving", as my UCSB colleague Dr. Garett Glasgow pointed out early in the case, most studies show that barriers on bridges serve only to divert suicidal behavior to other places. As ecology teaches, there is no simple "away", only other places. Suicidal people, unless they receive personal attention, find those places and choose other means to take their own lives.

In addition to these studies disproving the effectiveness of bridge barriers to save lives, as Caltrans specifically claimed, those of us who objected to the project learned that funds had been wrongfully diverted from monies set aside for "traffic safety" purposes and that the incident that had sparked the Sheriff's proposal to install barriers was the result of his failure and refusal to provide even minimal training to deputies in responding to suicidal individuals they encountered on the bridge. Also, Caltrans had sought to conceal the cost of the project, initially claiming a figure of $650,000 before we forced it to disclose that the cost would be closer to $4 million.

The barriers project was strongly supported by a local suicide-prevention group whose efforts I supported, except for their assertion that the barrier proposal would save lives. I was roundly condemned by it and its supporters for my refusal to pay heed to the argument that no amount of money was too much to spend in the hope that even one life could be saved.

As a careful student of the nature and kinds of "hope," I firmly and respectfully argued that this was a case of misplaced hoping at the expense of sacrificing the beauty of the bridge enjoyed by travelers year after year.

I was deeply saddened to receive hateful messages from members of families of persons who had committed suicide (none of whom had jumped from that bridge), as I understood the agony experienced by them as "suicide survivors." Of course, they wanted to save others from experiencing their pain, and I respected that motive. They were encouraged by the local suicide-prevention group not to believe Dr. Glasgow's conclusion that the project would not save lives.

Of course, Dr. Glasgow and I conceded the obvious fact that barriers might (they did not, as everyone later learned) prevent future jumps from the bridge.

I helped to organize and lead a group of several hundred people and several community groups under the name "Friends of the Bridge," and our efforts were successful in getting the State Transportation Commission to withhold funding for the project and to require Caltrans to stop trying to ram the project through without careful environmental review and a consideration of other ways to deter jumps from the bridge.

The latter was achieved through the legal efforts of the brilliant legal team of Marc Chytilo and Ana Citrin and the acumen of Superior Court Judge Tom Anderle. Marc was formerly EDC chief counsel, Ana one of my students at UCSB, and Tom one of the people in Santa Barbara I have long known and admired.

Among other active leaders of the fight to thwart the rush to deface the grace and beauty of the bridge were the directors of the Pearl Chase Society, John Woodward of the Santa Barbara County Landmarks Commission, and Jerry Jackman of the Santa Barbara Trust for Historic Preservation.

While we were successful in our legal efforts, the matter was ultimately determined by political considerations, not subject to review by the court or by the voters. The barriers went up, and soon after, a man climbed over them to jump to his death. As predicted, the barriers have had no discernible effect whatsoever on overall suicide rates in the community.

My friend Douglas Gillies, another former power lawyer who had come from San Francisco to practice law in the public interest in Santa

Barbara, helped me to get through the many disheartening moments along the way. We walked over the bridge together, he playing the trumpet, me a trombone, to keep up our spirits, and I made trips across it at many other times playing various other instruments I borrowed from the UCSB Music Department. The work took an enormous emotional toll on me, and such play was needed to help me endure it.

Marc playing trombone on Cold Spring Arch Bridge, 2009. *Photo by Paul Wellman.*

During this time, I was sometimes on the edge of burn-out, and I had to lean heavily on my family and friends to keep on. I am particularly grateful for the support of my Painted Cave neighbors Greg Farrell, high-voltage electrician turned wise guru, and his wife Rhonda, to whose doorstep I would come for solace and comfort during my darkest moments.

My heart continues to beat irregularly, but my cardiologist says it seems determined to carry me along and that I should follow it, which is great spiritual as well as medical advice, best taken when we find ourselves on the verge of losing heart altogether.

Consumer ≠ Citizen Culture

10

W hen I began my teaching career at UCSB in the 1970s, I invited my students to undertake a rigorous and heartful exploration into colliding worldviews about who people are and the nature of the world in which we're living. As I've mentioned, our human ancestors saw and behaved themselves as part of—and not apart from—the rest of the communities of life all around them. Theirs was first by necessity and then by purposeful intention a deeply conservative and fundamentally respectful ecological worldview.

Only in the last few moments of the time that humanity has been a part of the circle of life on the planet has a radically different worldview arisen, in a head-on collision with humanity's customary worldview.

That recent and radical worldview began taking form a mere 0.3 percent of the time since our first civilizations arose, and it threatens to bring human civilization to a sorry end by the conditions that it has engendered on the face of the planet.

The so-called "modern" worldview goes by several names. Here I will call it by two: the Man As Dominant (MAD) worldview and the Dog Eat Dog (DED) worldview. These ideas are based on two misperceptions concerning living reality, one stemming primarily from an ecologically uninformed tenet of Judeo-Christian religious belief, and the other from an ecologically uninformed scientific view of the complex processes of evolution of human and other species on the planet.

"Man As Dominant" (MAD) worldview

Moses or whichever man (no women need apply!) wrote in the Book of Genesis that God had commanded those who had been created in His image ("he" or "him" are the pronouns) "to subdue [the Earth] and have dominion over the fish of the sea, and over the fowl of the air, and over every living thing that moveth upon the Earth."

This idea was ecologically illiterate, a perfectly understandable fact. Moses also reported that God had commanded him "to replenish the Earth," a perfectly sensible requirement of good agriculture and husbandry practices of those times.

What got latched onto by Jewish and Christian theologians alike was not the sensible injunction to replenish the Earth, but the senseless ones to subdue and have dominion over the Earth.

Until Greek Orthodox Patriarch Bartholomew and Pope Francis came along in 1997 and 2015, respectively, to add their voices to that of Saint Francis of Assisi (c. 1181-1226) in calling for a saner view of the relationship between human beings and the rest of life on the planet, the MAD worldview held baleful sway over Western religious thought and belief.

It was to Santa Barbara, justly called the birthplace of the environmental movement in 1970, that Patriarch Bartholomew came to flatly declare, "Dominion is not domination" at the 1997 Symposium on the Sacredness of the Environment. To carry forth this defining message, members of the Interfaith Initiative of Santa Barbara County have convened the ECOFaith coalition, under the leadership of Ed Bastian, Mollie DeWald, Mark Childs, Kathleen Moore, Hymon Johnson, Art Cisneros, Ivor John and several others.

Happily, similar eco-interfaith groups are arising across the nation and around the world to carry forward the dawning of ecological enlightenment into religious realms. Prominent among these is GreenFaith, whose mission is to articulate and act upon the teachings of Judaism in relation to enlightened environmental stewardship and care of the living world.

In such an enlightenment of religious understanding, one can clearly see and powerfully confront the sheer madness of the MAD worldview notion that "Mars is our next home," as if the Earth were merely a disposable commodity. Such a notion is beyond mere nonsense. It is insanity on stilts.

At long last, the teachings of organized religion are coming into confluence with the ecological worldview: "Everything on Earth is sacred and nothing in or of it belongs to us, for we faithfully belong to all of it." Organized religion has begun to move joyfully along the path of ecological enlightenment.

My personal journey has been along a spiritual rather than a religious path. For me, the essential teachings of environmental thinkers and writers such as Rachel Carson, Aldo Leopold, E.F. Schumacher, Theodore Roszak, Wendell Berry, Amory Lovins, Paul Hawken, Thich Nat Hanh, Bill McKibben, Naomi Klein, Rebecca Solnit, among others, are profoundly spiritual in nature. They fuse in me with the teachings of Lao Tzu: "The way to do is to be," and of Ram Dass: "Be here now," in which I seek to come to center in present awareness.

Being loving leads effortlessly to doing that which is loving. Being respectful leads effortlessly to doing that which is respectful.

I came to my environmental awareness and ecological understanding "from the inside out" in this way.

Along my journey, I and other environmentalists have been accused from time to time of trying to start a new religion. That is simply not the case for me. Rather, I've been encouraging existing religions to start taking to heart the teachings of the ecologically enlightened Saint Francis of Assisi.

In the courtyard of the offices of the Environmental Defense Center is a statue of Saint Francis, called by many the patron saint of ecology.

For many religious leaders and followers, today the whole Earth is a church.

Regarding the "Dog Eat Dog" (DED) worldview

Charles Darwin simply got it wrong in positing the scientific notion that the fundamental driving force in the evolution of species is essentially competitive rather collaborative.

For all his efforts, he simply lacked a sufficient ecological understanding of how the world works, and so he wound up coming to a back-assward conclusion. Says who? A consensus of ecologically-informed scientists working in the field today. People led astray by Darwin owe an apology to dogs for jumping onto the "Dog Eat Dog" bandwagon and worldview. Dogs have far more sense than that.

It is beyond my professional competence as a lawyer to elaborate the details of this particular scientific comeuppance and profound clarification, but as a close student of both the law and history, I can happily report that the whole social Darwinist enterprise has also been turned on its head.

The social Darwinists sought to justify colonialism and the subjugation of so-called more "primitive" peoples, who they said were ill-prepared to competently manage their own lives and affairs. Thus, they said, it was "the white man's burden" to dispose of less-fit people and their wealth. Such a wrong-headed and pinch-hearted worldview provided post-facto justification for, among other atrocities, the genocide performed on the "savage" indigenous peoples who stood in the way of the western expansion of "white supremacy" across the United States.

By clearing today the dreadful muck of yesterday's social Darwinist enterprise, we may come to a clear understanding of how best we citizens in the so-called "developed world" can effectively work for justice for all and not merely out of self-interest.

So what do I mean by consumer ≠ citizen culture?

What I call "consumer culture" is the dominant culture we in the United States find ourselves in today, as a consequence of the consumptive economy that has so far been in place. It was purposefully created in the aftermath of World War II in order to achieve post-war economic recovery in a manner advantageous to the United States.

Of all the warring nations, the United States alone came through the war in a stronger economic condition than when the war began. Alone among our allies and enemies, we escaped the bombing and devastation of our cities and industrial infrastructure. Under the rubric "America: The Arsenal of Democracy," the United States achieved a full-employment economy based on the production of weapons and war material. The United States had emerged from the Great Depression into a condition of relative prosperity.

The nation's post-WWII economic and political planners huddled with the leaders of the most powerful corporations and came up with the Marshall Plan and similar programs in order to both achieve a seamless transition for a wartime to a peacetime economy and achieve the economic recovery of former allies and enemies as a basis for developing reliable trading partners and markets abroad.

However, when the former ally the Soviet Union moved aggressively to pursue its own interests in Europe and around the world, the political and corporate leaders of the United States came to see that a Cold War had come into being, between the competing ideologies and political economies of capitalism and communism.

When the Soviet Union detonated its first nuclear weapons, the reverberations rattled the windows at Hanford and in the offices of governmental and corporate office buildings across the United States. Abashed but unbowed, America's corporate and political leaders moved full speed ahead to demonstrate to their own people and to people around the world the superiority of a capitalist economy to provide an abundance of "consumer goods and services."

Henceforth, it was decided, the people of the United States should be made to think of themselves first and foremost as "consumers" rather than as citizens, the people of, by, and for whom the United States was created as a beacon of democracy. Citizens had to be made to believe that "it's the economy, stupid" to which to pay allegiance rather than to their democratic institutions of political governance.

Many far better-qualified and more astute observers have recounted the rise and consequences of consumer culture, and among them I recommend the account provided by Lizabeth Cohen in her exhaustively-researched and well-written book, *A Consumers' Republic: The Politics of Mass Consumption in Postwar America*.

Here is how she winds up in the concluding paragraph of the book:

"Even if we would prefer to decouple citizen and consumer, the best we may hope for is to turn this inheritance from the twentieth century to our advantage in the twenty-first. Taking nothing for granted, we can hold our mandate to be both citizens and consumers to the highest standards of democracy, freedom, and equality, dwelling not so much on whether we should simultaneously be citizens and consumers but rather accepting that, like it or not, we are. The question then becomes, United States citizen: consumer in what kind of republic?"

Lizabeth Cohen is a distinguished Professor of American Studies at Harvard University, and I intend to be a voice for the Earth in addressing her conclusion and closing question.

Given the perilous state of the global environment and its communities of life, of which we are a part, I'm committed to doing what I can to decouple "citizen" and "consumer" so that we can most appropriately and effectively act upon our environmental rights and responsibilities going forward.

I am grateful to Professor Cohen, with whom I do not fully agree, for helping me to understand more fully what we citizens of the Earth are called upon to do to break the grip of consumerism and the consumptive economy.

When Professor Cohen and other scholars of American Studies look back on the next several years to come, may they record and report that a turning point was reached, somewhere around the first quarter of this century, whereby citizens refused to be regarded and governed as if they were mere consumers or as anything other than as fully-empowered and responsive citizens.

They might report that a kind of consumer liberation movement had occurred, in which the term "consumer" was consigned to the trash bin of history.

May it be.

I have come to know for certain that I am the co-creator of my experience of life. What happened or is happening or may happen in my life has the meaning that I choose to make of it.

We are all the meaning-makers of our lives and our circumstances, and I believe that all of us have healing powers to bring to bear as we make our journeys amidst each other and the world or worlds in which we find ourselves.

What a thrilling experience it is to find myself—blind-spots, shortcomings and all—on a path of conscious evolution, and to find an ever-increasing number of others doing the same. I am fully conscious of the fact that I am no mere "consumer."

We are making our futures and histories as we create our meaning in the present moment. When we come to center in present awareness (into the place I call "presence") we may find ourselves in befitting gratitude and humility and possessed of remarkable powers of forgiveness, compassion and empathy. We may find ourselves to be fully fit to take our place as citizens rather than consumers, to shift the course toward which the human species is headed. Imagine a world in which people consider themselves as creative sources of beauty, grace, generosity, discernment and wisdom in the world.

The use of the word "consumer" is a step to dehumanize real people by putting them all into the same box to be dealt with *en masse*. Remember what took place when the label "savages" was affixed to indigenous people who were in the way of westward expansion. In California there was a reward paid for the cut-off ears of native men, women and children. We mustn't forget that the Nazis first dehumanized the Jews before sending them off in efficiently packed freight cars to their doom.

I believe that we're in an "all-citizens-on-deck" situation, and that we must act as citizens to save ourselves and the Earth community from the dehumanizing economic and political forces that seem hell-bent on consuming every single bit of Earth's bounty and then taking off for Mars or wherever.

How many rockets would it take over what period of time to bring that barren planet to life and to get an atmosphere and so forth in place to sustain people and other members of Earth's communities? Who would be on the passenger list? Who would decide?

Consumer culture is a toxic breeding ground for the virulent disease of *affluenza*. One catches the disease by swallowing the notion—the potion—that "more and newer is better" and that happiness is mostly about getting what you want to have from among a selection of items on sale.

To gain an understanding of the disease, my UCSB students and I watched and discussed the films "Affluenza" and "Escape from Affluenza" produced by Bullfrog Films in the late 1990s. The former is described by its makers as "a diagnosis of a serious social disease caused by consumerism, commercialism and rampant materialism that is having a devastating impact on our families, communities and the environment," and the latter as "showing audiences how to declare their independence from the epidemic of rampant consumerism and materialism ailing Americans and our environment by adopting practices of simple living."

A scene in one of them was particularly cringeworthy. It shows an advertising executive of a toy-making firm explaining why the depiction of aggressive, even violent behavior in advertising aimed at children is perfectly acceptable. "Aggressive behavior in pursuit of one of our products is a *good* thing," he blithely intones.

The Earth from outer space displays no sales tags or bar codes stamped anywhere on it. As I looked at my students, I didn't see consumers. I saw human beings, not human *have-ings*. I saw young Earthangels prepared to create the meaning of their lives through the exercise of their higher powers of citizenship and civic participation in accordance with their circumstances and opportunities.

At about the same time I noticed that many of them were wearing clothing with the brand labels prominently displayed on the outside rather than on the inside. I asked them, "How come?"

We talked about what was going on with that. We talked about whether people should have to pay for clothes like that or whether people should be paid to wear clothing providing advertising for its makers.

Near the beginning of all my classes I asked my students if any of them were consumers and requested a show of hands. I often had to repeat my question to encourage them to respond. With mostly quizzical expressions on their faces, first a few and then several and then most of the students raised their hand. "What kind of a trick question was this?", they wondered.

"Thank you," I said. "I don't see anyone in the room that I think of as a consumer." I would take off my glasses, wipe them clean, put them back on, and look again. "I only see my fellow citizens."

Inevitably we would consider the idea of "the power of consumers to vote with their dollars," and inevitably we would come to the conclusion that the expression of consumer preferences was a poor substitute for exercising the fuller powers of citizenship to oversee, through political governance, the operations of the economy—the same governance required to transform the consumptive economy into an ecologically sustainable one.

Over the years I've had the pleasure of running into a great many of my former students who took part in these conversations, and it has been a blessing to me to hear so many of them say how important it has been in their lives to embrace and act upon their role as citizens helping to run things, rather than consumers conditioned to let themselves be run over.

A consumer culture is profoundly effective at building upon itself. It has mastered the ability to manipulate desires through advertising. It's brilliant, and it works on human beings. A lot of people believe that the more you have the better you are. It's not true.

A popular bumper sticker that floated around awhile back said: "Live simply so that others may simply live."

My grandfather Edgar Furner was a man who lived simply and who provided the means for his customers to simply live during the Great Depression of the 1930s that continued to grip Utah communities into the early 1940s. He owned a small grocery store in Salt Lake City and generously allowed his customers to "put it on the tab" when they could not afford to pay right then for what they needed to provide for their families. In order to keep on providing for his customers in this way, he and his family tightened their belts to make ends meet, and he borrowed money from his bank to keep the business running to meet his customers' needs.

His customers paid what they could, but it wasn't enough for Grandfather Edgar to meet the bank's demands for full repayment strictly on time, and so the bank foreclosed on the business and got what money they could from it and then shut it down. Grandfather Edgar had to endure bankruptcy, an almost overwhelming agony for him, but he was anything but a bankrupt man.

I guess you could say that the "Story of Grandfather Edgar" was for me like the Book of Genesis may be for its believers. In the beginning, there was an extraordinary man who put the well-being of his community above his own self-interests and provided for his customers in their time of need. He was betrayed by money-changers doing business-as-usual, who put their own interests above those of this generous man and his people. The story of my grandfather is part of the gospel I have tried my best to adhere to during my life.

As a kid I enjoyed my second-hand stuff and liked to make use of all kinds of old things, as my grandparents did. But in the booming prosperity of the post-WWII years, my stepfather caught the affluenza virus and went nearly hog-wild in attempting to acquire as much stuff as he could in order to race to "keep up with the Joneses." Every other year he tried to scrape up the money to buy a new car (once a shiny new Edsel that was a lemon from the get-go; another year an awful new Plymouth the color of a hospital room). And every couple of years he uprooted us all to move to a house in a better part of town. He didn't have to do what he did; he simply had to, if you see what I mean.

I preferred the "waste not/want not" example of my grandparents. I didn't care a whit about what the Joneses were up to. As it happened, when I finally met a family of Joneses, they seemed to be living happy lives more like the way that my grandparents did.

The ethos of consumer culture is a grave but surmountable impediment to our coming to our senses in order to avoid the deadly consequences of letting ourselves be goaded into living beyond our means and beyond the limits of the world to sustain such behavior. Consumerism is spiritually toxic. It is a cancer on the body politic for which citizens are responsible trustees. It cultivates relentless anxiety in the lives of the people who get caught up in it, about having and taking care of stuff, and about having the latest models or versions of stuff.

At the core of consumer culture and the consumptive economy is the totalitarian ideology that everything in the world is for sale and that everyone in it can be bought for a price.

Those who have designed and operate the ultimately ruinous consumptive economy say, "Let the devil and future generations take hindmost!"

They think that they've figured out how best to run the whole show: as a corporatocracy rather than being in accordance with the principles and practices of constitutional governance. This corporatocracy has succeeded in persuading a majority of the United States Supreme Court to name corporations as "people," against all evidence that the drafters of the Constitution and Bill of Rights had no such intent whatsoever, understanding that real people are mortal and that corporations are merely business arrangements that can live on forever at the whim of their creators. Among the items on the list of things to be done by citizens today is to see that this daft decision is overturned.

What we could use now is a second emancipation proclamation, one to free people from their enslavement within consumer culture and the consumptive economy. Remember that it was in order to overthrow the human slavery-based political economy of the Confederacy that President Lincoln issued the Emancipation Proclamation. It is time for another one to overthrow the consumer slavery-based consumptive political economy that has remained in place for far too long.

We could also come up with a Pledge of Allegiance to the Whole Earth. We could pledge ourselves to live our lives as if the well-being and sustainability of the Earth's people and other communities of life matter.

To do so we could pledge ourselves to the practices of what I call "subversive frugality" in confronting the totalitarian ideology of consumer culture and the consumptive economy.

When I was in Nicaragua during the Contra War to attend one of the Fate of the Earth conferences convened by David Brower, I saw former supermarkets and grocery stores with very few items on their shelves. I needed toothpaste, and I had my choice of just one kind, in just a few tubes. What I found was sufficient to meet my need. Had I been at home, I would have been confronted by a far, far, far greater selection of brands and varieties of toothpaste from which to choose. Ditto for anything else on the overflowing shelves of a typical store in the United States.

How much is enough? Why has simple sufficiency been overwhelmed by this gluttony that seems to have taken hold?

The Sandinista Revolution was undertaken in order to throw off the yoke of political and economic domination by the United States and the dictatorial regimes that were its servants in governing the country. The Reagan administration was intent on the overthrow of the Sandinista government in order to force the return of Nicaragua to within its imperial sway. Millions of dollars derived from the secret sales of military arms to Iran were pumped to the Contra forces waging civil war on the new government.

In a very real sense the war that was waged by the United States and the Contras against the Sandinista government was a war between the competing ideals of the colonizing, consumptive economy of the United States and the ideals of the people of Nicaragua regarding their rights to choose their own sovereign political and economic arrangements, those they chose for themselves and were not compelled to swallow and endure.

When public interest lawyer Daniel Sheehan and others blew the cover off the secret arms sales, the Reagan administration was forced by Congress to withhold further support for the Contras, and the war came to an end. As a witness to some of the horror of that war, I rejoiced at the success of the Nicaraguan people to get out from under the colonizing yolk of the consumptive economy.

Do you want to be a radical today, at whatever age you happen to be? Then I suggest that you simply go about living within your means. Buy only what you really need, and do your best to make things last. You don't need all the stuff that you see when you walk into a store. You can have sufficiency.

If you can, grow some of your own food and consciously participate in your own sustenance in other ways. You know how much is enough for you to be happy and satisfied and well-nourished.

The meaning of wealth depends on your perspective. If you're not hugely in debt, and you have a sufficient place to live, food to eat, friends to laugh and play with and learn from and teach, then you're *rich*.

Debt in any amount imposes a degree of limitation on our choices in life. Huge debt, such as many of my students have faced by taking out educational loans, can literally be enslaving. In nearly all of my classes at UCSB I assigned what I called "Whole Life/Whole Earth" homework that required my students to keep careful track, down to the penny, of all of their income and expenses. My purpose was to help them to create and manage their own economies, keeping in mind the workings of both the consumptive economy and ecological economy of the whole Earth. I invited them to consider, personally, every day of the year, the consequences of their economic activities on others and the whole Earth.

So be *rich in your simplicity*, I say. In your frugality, be rich in relation to what you need to lead a happy life. Be rich in this *modest* way, then seek to enrich the experience of those people who look at you and see another way to live, a way to feel centered in gratitude rather than to be a rootless soul forced to be complicit in the consumptive economy.

For the least of things, we can be grateful. It's much more straightforward to do this when the array of things around you isn't so large as to be spiritually burdensome.

At the Earth Day Festival in Santa Barbara by the Community Environmental Council (CEC) there are on display a wide array of products and services by which to live and work and play in a sensible and frugal way. Such products and services are becoming available nearly everywhere in the country. Many of the best of them originated elsewhere. There is an emerging global marketplace which ecologically conscious citizens can help to widen and deepen by aligning their personal economies to it. Thus can citizens vote with their dollars to transform the consumptive economy into an economy that allows its citizens to live simply in order to help others and the whole Earth to simply live.

Does the consumptive economy have a future? Is it the same future that an aggressive cancer has in a body? It's a public health issue, as well as an economic and political one. Are the stresses imposed by the consumptive economy a factor in the cancer epidemic among people caught up in trying to buy well-being and happiness? Of course it is!

Teach your children well, that they are not what they have, that there is far more to life than merely having stuff. This issue is worth fighting for.

I believe that for the human species to survive, we who are here today and those of us who are coming must do all we can to overthrow consumer culture and the consumptive economy on which it is based.

Did you know that the word "consumption" was once used in medical circles to describe the deadly disease of tuberculosis? And that those afflicted with the disease were described as being "consumptive"? While we have made important strides in developing medical responses to the scourge of tuberculosis, we have not fully come to recognize the diseases that the consumptive economy causes to individuals, to communities and to the whole body politic.

On a spiritual level I believe that "we are one," and yet we are all naturally unique, with no two of us exactly alike, not even twins. We exist in a world of diversity. In fact, the science of ecology teaches that it is the diversity of a living system that is most essential to its stability and continued presence in the world.

Mono-cropping and other "simplifying" agricultural practices are destructive of system-diversity, and experience has shown that reliance on them leads to bankruptcy in the long term in many more ways than one. And it's the long term that we are required to think about if we wish our species to survive and flourish.

The consumptive economy commodifies everything in its path, pillaging natural diversity to homogenize people and affix barcodes to their foreheads that can readily be scanned for systematic tracking. Is this really for the convenience of the consumer? After all, don't unbidden messages pop up on our electronic devices, calling our attention to purchase and buy? Is this for our convenience? Is algorithmic data tracking of us really necessary? For whom? For what reason?

It's very important to resist the conformity of consumerism, to resist homogenization. There is an awful conformity in consuming culture, even though the attempt is made to create the impression that the choices are endless. That's an illusion, as is the impression that your choices of customized, "personalized" goods are manifestations of your unique personality. People start walking around as advertising billboards with all their brands showing on the outside of their clothes.

Beneath the veneer of consumer culture lies a wasteland of deadening conformity. And this deadening conformity contributes to narrow and shallow thinking in the civic sphere of life, what I have called the "body politic." Too much deadening conformity in our politics makes our democracy subject to falling into the hands of those who profit from pitting one party against the other in a partisan struggle for dominance or from creating just one party with two different names.

A careful look at the culture of consumerism clearly reveals that it undermines the culture of democratic citizenship and governance entrusted to our vigilant good-keeping by the Constitution and the Bill of Rights. These instruments are grounded in the self-respect, self-reliance and neighborly regard that we have for ourselves and our fellow citizens in preserving our union in the midst of the inevitable diversity of beliefs and opinions. In this light I ask you to consider the fundamental principle of the separation between church and state. I ask you to consider whether the consumptive economy has become a kind of church that threatens to dominate the state.

When people think of themselves as consumers, they confuse the blandishments of the consumptive economy with their civic duties. They are encouraged in this confusion by a wide variety of corporate and political mouthpieces. After the attacks of 9/11, President George W. Bush exhorted Americans, "I encourage you all to go shopping." It was a shameful moment for democracy in our country.

No amount of consumer spending can do more for the country than the work of well-informed citizens who vote and act in other ways to participate in the governance of the nation. Shopping carts full of goods cannot hold office and will never enact laws. There's a better way to participate than merely buying a bunch of stuff in order to keep the cash registers ringing so the consumptive economy can go on running on high.

There's the claim that we must buy more to support jobs, that all of our "livelihoods" are dependent on conformity with the demands of the consumptive economy. Yes, there is a clear relationship between spending and jobs, but the real question is what kind of spending and what kind of jobs we are talking about, as well as the ways we might improve the relationship by coming to an ecologically-centered economy that best honors and acts in light of that interdependent economic and political relationship.

Your freedom and security depend on my willingness to be a citizen, to inform myself about the issues, and to vote and participate in other ways in political governance. My freedom and security are likewise at risk unless you do the same, even though we may not agree with each other about many or most of the issues that are up for decision. But if I get all caught up in the throes of consumer confusion to the extent that I overlook my civic responsibilities to you, what then? Have I not left you and your loved ones in the lurch?

I hope that you would tell me so and would do what you can to get me to wake up and come to my senses. I hope that you would help me to do my part in our interdependent relationship. I hope you would remind me that my "worth" to you and your loved ones is infinitely greater when I act as a responsible citizen than when I get hung up in my false consumer identity.

Consumer culture has produced a situation in which a brutal money-grubber has arisen to become president and commander in chief. It is both ridiculous and terrifying. This is what consumer culture and the consumptive economy have come to. It's a good thing we are here to bring into being a more sane, just and ecologically-wise economy and to get bipartisan political governance up and running again.

A din of angry and hateful shouting is going on in the country right now. A powerful and appropriate response to angry shouting is to bring to bear the demonstration, the portrayal and the presence of peace. Peace on and with the Earth starts at home, where I am and where you are.

By becoming fully awake to our condition, we can stop fooling ourselves and allowing people to fool us, inviting foolishness to go on without end. Instead we can take it upon ourselves to practice remaining at-center and in peaceful presence, while working like the dickens to overthrow the consumptive economy.

It's best to take bold steps calmly. We need a revolution in our own conduct toward our Earth home and toward each other. As consumers, people are divided. Yet as Earthling citizens, we can be united!

If we have learned from our current situation (and from history), we know that certain people have used our differences in order to manipulate and divide us for the sake of increasing their power. We do indeed have our differences (a good rather than a bad thing), and we don't need to agree on everything. We can experience our inevitable differences in peaceful ways, and that peace can derive from better understanding of our differences. Understanding doesn't require agreement, even on the really big questions.

We have no choice in a nuclear age, on a crowded planet. We don't have the luxury of indulging in violent confrontations with each other that drain our resources and waste opportunities.

It's our duty to teach our children well about who others are, to show them that those others are just like ourselves in their citizenship. We are all citizens of the Earth, regardless of our skin color, religion, gender or our economic worth.

However, we do all participate in an economy; not the narrow economy, but the grand, ecological economy. We partake of a planet-wide ecology that is a full-employment economy, a system within which there's work for everybody. It's the only truly sustainable economy: the economy of caring for the planet, of giving as much as we take, in balance.

Giving and taking in equal measure supports healthy relationships at every scale. We exist in a field of relationships. This is the knowledge that the science of ecology reveals to us. We move in a sea of relationships, and in those relationships we conduct transactions and exchanges. As human beings within this field, we have the capacity to help one another and to uplift one another.

On Despair

11

For the past 15 years or so, I've found myself teetering on the edge of despair, where I've encountered many of my friends, companions and colleagues, also struggling. We've won important victories and suffered agonizing defeats. Our hearts have been buffeted and broken and our resolve has sometimes been shaken. What's to be done with our heartbreak and despair?

To understand and work through my own heartbreak at the continuing predations of the consumptive economy upon people and the ecological community of the whole world, I had to go deeply within myself to examine closely my innermost motivations and expectations. Why was I taking my work so seriously? Was I taking myself too seriously? Was I spiritually and emotionally fit for such a hard slog? How often and to what extent was I sufficiently awake, or was I walking around half or fully asleep? Did my efforts really matter much at all?

When I was a young man, thousands of men, mostly men like me, were fighting in Vietnam. At the same time, many men and women were fighting segregation and injustice in America's Deep South and in other places across the country. All of them were putting their lives on the line. I was not among them. I was in law school trying to figure out if I wanted to become a lawyer and, if so, what kind.

By the time I saw the whole Earth from outer space, I had become a well-trained lawyer and fallen in love, not with the law but with a woman with whom I wished to have children.

When I saw the Earthrise image for the first time, I fell head over heels in love with the Earth, a love more vast and intense than any love I have ever known, and when I got Pete McCloskey's call, I threw myself headlong and heart-first into work that I hoped to do for all of my life.

"Earthrise" from Apollo 8, December 24, 1968. *Photo by Bill Anders/NASA.*

When I entered the fight, my fighting skills were honed and at the ready, and I was hoping that in my lifetime, most people would come to hold the Earth in deep reverence. I was hoping for too much, and it was that hope that made me vulnerable to disappointment and despair when the forces of the consumptive economy rallied themselves to counter the efforts of the environmental movement that I had helped to get underway.

My teeth are all my originals, but it felt like all of them had been knocked out by the blows I suffered when my efforts and those of my companions went to naught, and when Whole Earth consciousness seemed a chimera destined to fade and disperse.

Yes, I had hoped for too much to take place in my lifetime. No, I have not given up on hope. In order to continue my work in good spirit and fine tune, I've found it necessary to move *beyond* hope as a source of motivation to keep on moving forward in the face of disappointment and despair.

It's been a tall order for me to face. Vivid in my mind were the words I heard Wendell Berry say during one of his visits to Santa Barbara when I was asked whether or not he was hopeful as he went about his work.

"Isn't hope a virtue? If you haven't got any, well, you surely should find a way to get some."

Like many, if not most of us, I was afraid to fully face and get to the roots of my despair. For years, I wallowed in and at the edges of my despair, and I licked my wounds until I was tired of their bitter taste.

During the unraveling of my second marriage of many years, I felt caught up in a torpor of hopelessness and I felt myself sinking to the bottom, and when we decided to live apart, I bottomed out.

The rugs on which I had stood, wobbling so long, were pulled from under my feet, and I had no choice but to get better footing somehow. I had to decide what meaning to make of the rest of my life. I was at a fork in the road, and I really had no choice but to fully face and confront the roots of my despair and find a way through to a stronger sense of presence in order to keep on serving my purpose. As many wise traditions seek to teach us, "necessity is the mother of invention."

I did what was needed to invent myself anew.

What freed me up to undertake and accomplish my task centered on embracing both my ignorance and my certainty: my ignorance about how my efforts could ever lead to the sustainable world I envision, and my ignorance of what will actually come to pass in the future; the certainty of my gratitude and love for the Earth, for the opportunity to be and do what I can in service to the Earth so long as I live, right up to the moment I die and my spirit moves on.

As a young athlete I always practiced beautifully, because during practice I had no fear of failure. As a football quarterback none of my errant passes in practice would lead to defeat in real games, and in baseball none of my strikeouts in practice carried such weight either. But in real games, my fear of failure too often kept me from doing my very best.

I know now that failure is a fact of life, best regarded not as a sin, but as something that gifts us new perspectives of how to be and what to do better.

Failure can lighten up the shadows. It can illuminate opportunities that had been hidden in the darkness, just out of sight. Failure can be a creative place, if we open ourselves to what failure can show us. Each failure can shine a light on another aspect of what was or might have been missing that would have allowed for success.

When we're playing "the big game" in our lives, we confront failure on a regular, even daily basis. The game we are playing is a big one indeed. It is a game in which getting a handle on our fears will help us to keep doing our best in the face of failure, disappointment and despair.

I want so much to live among others who are in reverence for the Earth, and so I'm constantly devastated to find myself in the midst of consumer culture and the consumptive economy. When I accept my ignorance and come to gratitude and humility, I can muster compassion and forgiveness for myself and my shortcomings. If I could not do this, I would be crippled.

During meditation on the beach one day, what I call a "heart's breath song" came to me. As I inhaled, the word "forgiven" whispered itself into my heart and inner being, and as I exhaled I heard my heart and inner being whisper "forgiving."

After several minutes of this I felt bathed in healing light and energy. I was filled to the brim with gratitude for the gift of this experience, and it has become one of my core practices of gratitude and grace which bring me to center and to presence.

Such practices lift me out of the pits of disappointment and despair in which, idealist that I am, I'm prone to stumble into from time to time. They help me to recognize the beauty and abundance that abound and are available to draw upon, to move forward in good spirits in the company of people I love and who love me.

My practice is to *come to center throughout the day*. What that means to me is to call my own awareness to be present in the present moment, what Ram Dass called "being here now."

In presence, I abide in conscious awareness. It's a means of awakening and remaining awake, of fending off apathy, torpor and discouragement. It's a means to quiet anger and dissolve fear. It's a means to come to balance, acceptance and clarity, to choose what we want our purpose to be and to align our actions to fulfill it as best we can, through thick and thin.

It's so easy to get distracted by illusion, and distraction is a stealthy foe. Distraction lies at the heart of mindless consumerism. Instead, let us be mindful.

When we're present and noticing being here now, we become awake to the complex field of relationships within which we exist.

It's wondrous to realize that our understanding is limited compared to our far-reaching entanglement in the web of life. We can feel profound humility in the face of complexity. Life isn't an illusion but rather a circumstance about which we manufacture illusions.

One of the illusions we manufacture is the idea that our actions are of no consequence. Our actions *always* have consequences; some intended and some unintended.

Why not just pour this waste on the ground, in the lake, in the river, in the pond, in the ocean, into the air? Let's put it "somewhere else."

But my "somewhere else" is someone else's "here." In reality, there is no "somewhere else."

We're all in the soup together, in the stew, in the pot, where things are heating up. There is no "away."

Marc, age 8. *Photo courtesy of Marc McGinnes Archives.*

When I was a boy riding beside Grandfather Edgar in his old car with our windows wide open, I once opened a Baby Ruth bar, offered him a bite, and tossed the wrapper out the window and away.

Grandfather pumped the tired brakes to a stop, turned off the ignition, and said to me, "I will wait here while you go back and pick up that wrapper and put it in your pocket until we get home."

"Go lightly on the land, and by all means don't litter." This was the message he delivered unspoken, since in my surprised gaze at his face I saw that his lips were unmoving. He was a picture of kind patience.

Our challenge is to widen ourselves to include the whole world and to be a respectful part of it. When we know this about ourselves, we don't make use of the world as a garbage bin. We don't try to get rid of things by carelessly putting them on or into the land or waters or air or fire. From these four elements we ourselves have come to be.

We are challenged to turn the heat down, both for our climate and within ourselves, and I believe that we have the capacity to do so if we can come to our senses. Cooler heads than those who have steered the consumptive economy into such a ditch are needed in order to lead the effort to cooler ways to proceed in the future. The path to cooling things down will not be industrial or technological. It will require a shift in and further evolution of human consciousness.

We are consequential, and we could gratefully embrace that obvious fact of life. We may pray, each in our own way, to be of service in leading our lives. We may pray, each in our way, to have the courage it takes to fulfill such a commitment.

I know that my prayers are essential in my process of making meaning of and in the world. In one way or another, I pray all the time these days.

We can choose to be citizens. Whole Earth consciousness and citizenship is achieved through an ongoing practice of choosing to gratefully and humbly serve the needs of the larger Whole Earth community.

It's a process, and the process begins with choosing to be in conscious awareness. Choice is a subject explored extensively by philosophers. Like my fellow humans, I often seem to make the choice to avoid this state of mindfulness, as one temptation or another leads me to choose to exist on a lesser plane, to narrow down onto something I desire, something I think I need. For me, it takes daily practice to keep awake and on task.

Tree hugging has become one of my favorite of these practices. If you've ever done so, you'll understand why. If you haven't, you're in for a treat. Trees are possessed of wonderful powers, and to come into grateful intimacy with them has been both uplifting and grounding, and much more.

Marc and an old friend in Alameda Park, Santa Barbara, 2018. *Photo by Isaac Hernández.*

At our best, we humans are kind and compassionate to each other. At our worst, we murder and enslave. Speaking for myself, at my worst, I fall asleep, I forget who I am and what I'm for. At my best, I am an Earthangel, alive to my capacity for gratitude and in love with the whole Earth.

One can feel overwhelmed by despair, such despair that there doesn't seem to be a way out. New diagnosable conditions are being defined in response to this suffering: climate-anxiety, eco-grief, eco-anxiety.

It's a new reason to feel bad, a different condition from anything most people living in "modern" society have ever confronted before. There are support groups and eco-grief pills. A new fear arises: that the climate goes into chaos and we can't depend on it to be the cornucopia of all that consumption. Then what?

Chief Joseph of the Nez Perce Nation had no choice but to surrender his body and the bodies of his people to "the white man's way." Was it not what has now been named "eco-grief" that wracked his heart, mind and spirit as he was forced to do so?

Maybe the consumption economy is falling apart. The way to get through and not be pulled under by grief is to make the transition to more simple and respectful living. The choice-point is now here, and becoming more and more clear.

Many people have come to me to share their worries about the future. It is a blessing for which I am grateful. We share our fears so we can better get a handle on them, to keep them from overwhelming us. "Yes," we say to each other, "it's scary."

At this point, many of my students with whom I've huddled in this way have said, "If only everyone would wake up and see what's happening, then we all could…."

In one way or another, I would say to them that I was quite sure that "everyone would not" and that "we all could not" do anything in one way or another about the future.

What kind of help was that for me to offer to anyone in distress about the future, especially to a young person?!

Into the quiet that followed my saying these words, I would say, "On the scale of the problems we're dealing with, I think that we may be one hundred percent certain that *everyone* and *we all* will never do or not do anything. In our *diversity* we should not hope to achieve *unanimity*, as that would be to hope for an *impossibility*, given the scale of the conditions."

To get through our fears and to keep on with our work we need to avoid being diverted by misplaced hopes and impossible dreams.

All that is needed is a critical mass of people working within any human population to bring about a shift in the beliefs and behavior of most of the members of their wider community; most but never all, and I think that is a good thing. Hoping for the impossible is not only self-defeating, it is a toxic pollutant in the environment.

We don't know what's going to happen. So let's start by accepting that as true. We don't know. That comes first.

Secondly, we fear what might happen. Okay, we can count that as true too.

Third, since we know that we don't know what will happen and have accepted that fact, we can decide if we are going to let either our fears or our hopes distract from our efforts to bring into being a critical mass of people who think and behave like us in order to move away from overconsumption.

So, knowing that we don't know is the place to begin. That's the place to build upon. From there, you may see yourself as the sacred being that you are. You may see yourself as this beautiful, luminous person here in the present, knowing that you don't know.

And what *do* we know? That we are a part of everything. That we are a part of our friends, that we have good in us and that we don't have to be perfect to be okay. That we are a part of a movement that will build the critical mass needed to transform from overconsumption into balance.

Build upon your practices of gratitude and humility. Be present. Be centered. Be of brave heart and frisky spirit. Focus on forgiveness. Commit to forgiveness of your own failures and the failures of others. Commit to gracefully seeking and receiving the help that you need. Honor all of the connections and relationships that sustain you. And then work as hard as you can for the world you are determined to bring into being.

It is clear to me that gratitude is essential to our work. Gratitude is its own reward. As a state of consciousness, gratitude begets reverence. As I see it, we either come to reverence or we and much else comes to bust.

Whatever you may believe about how it is we came to be here and what this lifetime is about, you can be sure that if you're here, that this is where you belong on your journey. And here we are on this magnificent gem in space, resident on a planet with a gentle moon, and the sun as our star at just the right distance from us to be nurturing to us and the other forms of life that arise here.

Rights and Response-abilities

12

At one time, the curriculum in most if not all of the high schools across the United States required the study of civics by everyone who hoped to graduate in good standing. There was also a course in home economics at most high schools. Both of those courses remain important today as a means of helping young people to resist and overcome the predatory blandishments of the consumptive economy and consumer culture.

The teaching of Whole Earth citizenship and economics could be a priority throughout the entire K-12 curriculum. It would make a huge difference in the students' lives and for the whole world. We can see glimmerings of light that let us know that this is beginning to happen.

One of the places that this has been going on for many years is the Santa Barbara Middle School. Its founders were in Whole Earth consciousness when they brought it into being in 1977, the year that others of us, coming from the same place, created the Environmental Defense Center. Throughout the 41 years of its existence, Santa Barbara Middle School (SBMS) has had women and men as Earthwise teachers and mentors to two thousand or so students, eager to discover their place in their communities. On arduous bike trips and hikes and paddles, the students experience the natural world as a part of their classrooms, and they go on to teach others, including their families, what they're learning.

Adding up the many family members and friends, you can figure that the teachers and students of SBMS have helped tens of thousands of their fellow citizens to become Earthwise and act accordingly.

My former wife Kathy Snow served for many years on the SBMS staff. Both of my children, Skye McGinnes and Zach McGinnes, and both of my grandchildren, Helena McGinnes and Larkin McGinnes, have gone there. It has been a blessing for me to be invited to speak to the SBMS

Marc and his grandchildren Larkin, Chloe and Helena McGinnes (left to right), 2018.
Photo courtesy of Skye McGinnes.

community many times over the years, usually on Earth Day, and to have
gone on a few of the bike trips when I was younger.

Each Friday, I rise in time to join the sunrise circle that the 9th graders
lead, where students and family members come to center in presence
together. I hope to continue this practice right up to my end. Even when
I'm not able to be there and after I'm gone, my spirit abides in the circle.

Who of us will commit to sharing and practicing this kind of Earthwise education as a part of our work together?

Who will in this way bring us to our senses about who we are, to share
about our powers to understand the workings of dutiful governance and
the workings of long-term, sustainable economies at all scales? If you're
looking for meaningful work, this may be it for you.

Who needs seed money to start a new Earthwise school or to suitably
revise the existing curriculum? Where public schools are concerned,
might not this become a top priority for us as taxpayers?

In my high school civics course we learned, among many other
important things, that "we, the people" are citizens endowed by the Constitution with civil rights with which to perform our duties to country and
our fellow citizens in the communities to which we dutifully belong. We
are all well-conditioned to accept the notion of having a duty to country,

but amazingly, we so often fail to see the mirrored relationship whereby we owe a duty to the whole world.

It's the whole Earth that makes a person possible. We did not make it. It made each and every one of us. It's far from "woo-woo" to see the Earth as mother to us all, from whose womb we all came into being, and to whose embrace our bodies will return.

The whole Earth has conferred upon each of us the very right to live. Each breath we take is a gift. Each breath we give contributes to the holistic and holy workings of the whole Earth. Surely it's within our powers as people to see clearly our right relationship with the whole Earth and with each other.

In bringing into being the Santa Barbara Declaration of Environmental Rights, we sought to teach that citizens have the right to live in a livable environment and that such a right is among our other *civil rights* guaranteed by the Constitution. Our *civil responsibilities*, including contributing to the maintenance of a livable environment, received less emphasis and more neglect.

The Santa Barbara Declaration of Environmental Rights is a reflection of its time and place, where citizens, not long before the blowout, had been repeatedly denied even the right to speak at public hearings before federal officials in opposition to what seemed to them to be risky operations that would do great harm if not carried out with adequate care. It was a time to focus powerfully the rights of citizens to be heard within the workings of democratic governance regarding activities that posed the danger of environmental damage and abuse.

If I were I to write a similar document today, I might be inclined to call it a Declaration of Environmental Rights and Response-abilities. At the present time, I think it's vital to put greater emphasis on what most schools have forgotten to teach: that we have civic responsibilities to perform, if we hope to preserve our civil rights.

Our democratic system has been designed to be responsive to the people, but that can become wrangled into an authoritarian corporatocracy. If citizens can be made to shirk their civic responsibility to ensure that the government faithfully obeys the constitutional demand to preserve and promote the public health, safety and welfare, they will have badly impaired their civil rights. They will have done damage to their *abilities to respond*, their *response-abilities*, yielding them to those who are prepared to purchase the political process for their own economic and political ends.

This has already happened and it's going on now. The powerful corporate interests who have designed the consumptive economy have been able to secure a firm grip on the whole political process.

During my teaching years at UCSB, I invited my students and my colleagues, and on several occasions, gatherings of parents and campus officials to consider the relationship between civic responsibilities and civic response-abilities. None told me that they had ever heard the latter word until then. I think it should be in the next edition of the Oxford Dictionary.

While responsibilities are duties, response-abilities are rights.

If we can't respond to something, then we might have to lump it or leave it, but where does that leave us? Our legal and political systems have not been designed to *force* people to use their rights. We have the *right to respond* to the conditions of our lives, and it is by using our response-abilities that we do so.

Here I must insert something I see to be advisable. For the privilege of operating a motor vehicle, I believe it is proper to require that all who wish to exercise that privilege must regularly exercise their privilege of voting. Will that lead to problems? Of course it will, as every action has consequences. I think we can figure out an appropriate way to move forward on this in view of the good it may do.

Voting is just one of our civic response-abilities, and we have others which we can exercise on a daily basis, such as our rights to appear before all local, state and federal governmental bodies and administrative agencies to advocate for our own and the public interests that are involved in the decisions to be made. Unless citizens exercise these ongoing response-abilities, the decision-making process will be dominated by those who profit from keeping the consumptive economy on its ecologically destructive course.

During my years at UCSB I said to the university community, from the Chancellor to the entering freshman students and all in between, that

I think that the most important educational mission of the university is to educate citizens to recognize and act upon their response-abilities, and that these response-abilities are of a personal nature.

I am a citizen relating to a government that is of, by and for the people. This means that matters of public health, safety and welfare are, for me, matters of personal concern. I take personal responsibility for that part of the public health, safety and welfare to which I can contribute by exercising my personal response-abilities.

At the present time we and the whole world are suffering the harm being brought about not only by the consumptive economy but by the consumptive political practices of powerful interests who designed it and are doing their utmost to keep it humming along in devil-may-care efficiency.

Our political system has become consumptive with the vast monies pumped into the political process in order to make citizens believe that their duty to country compels them, first and foremost, to be good consumers rather than good citizens. Vast monies maintain a system of political prostitution whereby corporations are permitted to pump vast sums of money into the campaigns of political candidates and office-holders who are beholden to the agenda of the consumptive economy.

Thus has arisen in our country the scourge of corporatocracy that has damaged our democracy and which threatens to drown it in a sea of money.

Neither of the two major political parties in the country are immune from this, but at the moment one of them seems fully hell-bent on maintaining its grip on power in this way. This party seems terrified by the attempt of the previous administration to put a check on efforts to degrade democracy in favor of domination by corporate interests. By any means possible, by hook or by crook, these interests and their political prostitutes seek to convince citizens that they must submit, must unconditionally surrender, to sticking to their assigned roles of obedient consumers.

Such submission, such abandonment by citizens of their democratic rights/response-abilities and their responsibilities, enables the rise of brutal measures to keep people on the assigned consumerist take and to keep them sated with stuff so they won't step out of line in political resistance.

Remember: the Nazi regime took brutal measures against any person who refused to "obey orders," the primary one of which was the command to set aside and surrender up to the state all "personal responsibility" and to think and act as they say first. We know what happened as a consequence of that.

"I was only doing my duty," was an excuse for barbarism and genocide.

Whenever people are pressed to believe that they need not and must not take "personal responsibility" for their actions, they are being pressed to give up their civil rights/response-abilities with which to carry out their civil responsibilities. Down that road lies authoritarianism and its terrors.

It seems clear to me that some political leaders in the country want to take us all in that direction. They claim that it would really "make America great again." They disparage efforts to check their efforts as "witch hunts," and they encourage violence against those who resist their party line.

It is high time for us to come to center, into full presence, in the face of what is going on here now. This is no time for meek submission. We are in an all-citizens-on-deck struggle to determine the direction of the country going forward, and it is no time for any of us to shirk our personal responsibilities and response-abilities to participate in civic life.

The decision of George Bush, Dick Cheney, Donald Rumsfeld, Condoleezza Rice and other members of their gang to invade Iraq in 2003 kicked off a brutal bloodbath throughout the Middle East that is still in motion, at a cost of several trillions of dollars and close to a million lives. The invasion was undertaken in the attempt to assure the smooth running of the consumptive economy and its political servants, all consequences be damned.

If we had pursued our legitimate national interests in the Middle East, using the far better, wiser means of diplomacy, we and our brothers and sisters everywhere would be living in a saner and safer world today. Instead, we find ourselves in a state of continuous war.

The wars that are being waged inflict a stupendous burden of fear. Wars are fought over fear, because of fear, and in fear. And when war subsides in exhaustion or surrender, the fear doesn't disperse. It solidifies.

Military victory or victory through military force is an oxymoronic phrase. Today, the international ties between nations are so varied and many that the concept of winning and losing itself is deeply flawed. You can't win by destroying the enemy when you also hope to rebuild them in your own image. There is no victory, not really.

It is a requirement of justice that brute force not be allowed to govern. My knowledge of this comes from having lived in a family that really did seem to me, growing up, to be a brutal dictatorship, where any deviation from the will of the dictator resulted in violence and humiliation.

And in my wider social world, I grew up fighting. In the community I grew up in, if you wanted to be a leader among the young men there, you had to fight. You actually had to put your fist into somebody's face and feel yourself get hit by somebody else's fist. This was a rite of passage.

So, I learned how to fight, and I learned when and when not to fight. You can fight not only with fists, but with laws and ideas.

I grew up in a national security community where we produced nuclear weapons. We knew that we were targeted, so I wanted to step up and be a peacemaker, the US Ambassador to the Soviet Union.

I studied modern European history, learning about what happened between the wars. People were angry, belief and faith in institutions fell away, and it was a tumultuous and violent era. Moderate voices were shouted down by people both on the right and the left. The center could not hold. It was seen as old and discredited. There's the same feeling today of widespread dissatisfaction with and disdain for political and judicial institutions.

What can one do? As old Lao Tzu would say, that depends on who one chooses to be.

I believe that our spirits have chosen to be here now in our bodies so that we may be of service to each other and the Whole Earth community. In our heart-minds we can choose to be in such service through our participation in the political processes that are designed for that very reason. Service is what we are here for, and we have all the resources that are needed immediately at hand.

Let's get with it. There's no time to lose.

Heartsongs of Courage

13

One of the reasons I stopped teaching regularly was that, having hoped for too much, I lost hope. Not only had I hoped for too much in the future, I was caught up in hoping backwards into the past, and that dreadful combination had driven me off-center and out of the present.

I no longer felt I could be an authentic source of inspiration to my students and colleagues. My purpose had been to be an inspiring presence. I came to a place along my path where I became dispirited, where I looked into the abyss of despair. I was seething with a kind of sour anger born of disappointment, rather than the clean, bright, clear resolve that is needed to sustain the kind of work that is my purpose.

For some time now, I have been thinking a lot about hope, and have considered its uses and misuses as deeply as I am able. Is hope needed? Is it really a virtue, and to what extent can it actually be a burden? I challenged myself to think anew about hope, think differently, to entertain other ideas about something I had been taught one should always have, no matter what.

A couple of years ago, when I was in the midst of seeking a better understanding of hope, I dropped into the CEC offices to speak with my friend Sigrid Wright to discuss a couple of CEC's projects and to catch up with each other. Her eyes lit up when I began talking about my inner wrestlings about hope and despair, and she promptly performed one of the miracles that makes her the Earthangel that she is for me and so many others.

"Have you seen this?" she asked as she held out a book. "It has been helpful to me."

The book she handed to me was *Active Hope: How to Face the Mess We're in without Going Crazy* by Joanna Macy and Chris Johnstone. I hadn't come across it, but I had met Joanna years before and had read several of her other writings. I thought of her as a medicine woman, delivering messages of surpassing wisdom and grace. I had once participated, along with David Brower and others, in one of the "Council of All Beings" sessions that she conceived of and led for many years in several places around the country.

As I took the book in my hand, it seemed to open itself up to just the page I was meant to see first. Had Sigrid performed some kind of feat of kinetic ventriloquism? The words my eyes fell upon concerned the Earthrise photograph that I saw and that had knocked me into Whole Earth consciousness so long ago. I read the words of astronaut Bill Anders who had taken the photo. "We came all this way to explore the moon and the most important thing is that we discovered the Earth."

Everything about *Active Hope* is familiar to me, especially the role of *centering in gratitude* and the knowledge that we must be and act as citizens to work together to confront the craziness of the consumptive economic and political system.

Within a few weeks, I submitted a proposal to teach a seminar that I called "Hope That Works" during the Spring 2017 term for the UCSB Environmental Studies Program, and I was enthusiastically approved. The seminar centered on a consideration of the ideas set forth in *Active Hope* and readings I selected to accompany it, together with discussions with various members of the faculty concerning their views about the place of hope in their work and lives.

This step was so important for me! It reaffirmed my duty as an Earthling elder to express my conviction, once again, that we are much more powerful than the forces of materialism and greed that have brought about the consumptive economy and the culture of consumerism and their politics.

Standing in gratitude, being willing to commit, and then going forth in good spirit, with determination, makes us more powerful to those who have made their commitments to doing business as usual.

I feel so grateful to have recovered this sense of possibility in my life. I was 75 at the time, pretty old. I was not afraid of dying, but I didn't want to die unless fully awake at the moment.

I think it may have been a line or two from Carlos Castaneda about the presence in life of "death looking over our shoulders" that caused me to declare my preference out loud; "Not just yet."

Some kinds of hope are well worth avoiding. One kind enables a con game to be played upon people: get their hopes up and exert some control on their behavior. We have to help each other to get through the tricky ways of this kind of hope. And there is cowardly hope, which is merely trying to wish away problems without performing any work. Cowardly hope is toxic and very dangerous at a time when we need to face fear and deal with it. Problems can't be hoped away. It takes focused action to make things happen.

Hopes that technology can save us from ourselves have led us astray into believing that the gadgets can replace us and that it might be a good idea to gadgetize our bodies themselves. Dreams of becoming immortal have recently been voiced by some of the moguls of Silicon Valley.

It's a waste of time to linger in unrealistic escapist hopes, illusions and fantasies—which brings to mind James Watt, Reagan's Secretary of the Interior. Watt hoped that Jesus would be arriving before the next election and thus didn't seem to see the point of taking his duties seriously in the meantime. I wonder what Jesus would have said to the Secretary had he arrived and found him in that paralyzing and defeatist state of mind?

When I see myself in presence, I realize that I no longer need any hope at all to motivate me to continue my work in the present. The world I want to live in has not yet materialized, and yet I'm still alive, standing with a wounded but unbroken heart, seeing the prospect of my beautiful children and grandchildren living in a world that is new and bright for them.

Rather than trying to restore my hope, I saw that my task was simply to come to presence more fully. In that state, I saw that what I needed most was the courage to keep at my work in the face of knowing that I didn't know how things would work out for my loved ones and my Whole Earth community.

As I sought to buck up the courage to continue my work of seeing into being what I wanted, an inner voice asked, "Do you believe that the future exists outside of the present? You might do well to consider deeply this question."

When I am in presence now, I see that I had become confused by my success in "seeing into being," with things happening as I wanted them to. As a young baseball player I practiced this idea, hitting a homerun in games that had not yet happened; I practiced "seeing into being" the Environmental Defense Center and a number of other things.

These successes caused me to think that I was reaching somehow into the future that normally lay outside the boundary of the present. They caused me to think too little about the vastness of the present and to learn that the present is the one and only time/space there really is.

My confusion had gotten me off-center and off balance, and I had for too long been caught in hopes and expectations about the future.

When I heard Ram Dass's message to Be Here Now, I thought that I fully understood it. I was mistaken in my belief about it then, when I was younger. Now I think I understand it better, if not fully. Now I'm content to see that everything I saw into being happened in the present, and that the present is the only place to abide and work and play in, until there is no time/space at all.

What anchors me now is the knowledge that all of the work I've done was done in the present, and that all of my memories of having done so occur in the present, and that whatever of my work that might be carried on by others can only be done in the present.

I now proceed beyond hope to work in the present. I also understand and respect the place of hope in the lives of others, the place of hope that works.

Now, in presence, with the future in mind but having placed it where it belongs, expecting nothing to happen *there*, I can proceed with my work and help others proceed with theirs in the here/now.

My students and I came to see that hope has a role to play. We learned how to avoid the kinds of hope that can be self-defeating and the kind of hope that propels us to keep on working in the face of disappointments and defeats.

By coming to center and into presence, we are best able to come to the kind of detachment that many wisdom traditions teach. In Buddhist thought, the source of all suffering is one's attachment to that which is not real in the present. Whatever one thinks or feels about the past or the future is not real in the present, and the challenge one faces is not to get wrangled up in regrets, fears, dreams and so forth concerning them. To do so is to be attached to them and to suffer needlessly over one's illusions in the present.

Detachment is not achieved through any amount of distraction. Detachment is not merely taking one's mind off of anything; rather, it's a means of putting all things into appropriate perspective. Detachment does not take those who pursue it away from their concerns for others and for the whole world; on the contrary, it enables them to move forward into action most effectively. There's no single means by which to achieve this or any other kind of deep detachment. You can get all the help you need to find one or more strategies that work for you, if you commit to doing so.

Commitment and detachment are ways of being that are not in opposition to each other. They are in complementary relationship with each other in this way: it takes firm commitment to pursue the practices by which to achieve and maintain this kind of detachment, and it takes such detachment with which to make and maintain our firm commitments.

I've mentioned how my commitment was shaken by becoming too attached to the fruits of my labors. I forgot how to free myself of my attachments to things I was trying to see into being, as if trying to jerk the future into the present, where everything only happens in due course.

I think that courage is what's most needed. Like the word that describes it, courage is one of our heart's response-abilities, and like everything else that is worthwhile or essential, it takes work to keep it in good tune. It takes courage to get us to rise to our feet when we're knocked flat in the disappointment of our hopes and what we believed were our best efforts. In takes courage to keep keeping on when you look down and see some of your teeth on the ground after being clobbered in the mouth.

It takes courage not found in a shot glass or in any substance at all, except the whole substance and spirit of our being, to keep on doing what we believe that we're here for. It takes courage to secure ourselves to the mast when the ship of our purpose seems about to flounder and go under in a howling gale. It takes courage to remain afloat and swim to shore if that should happen and then to find our purpose again when we get to the shore.

Words to this effect were my final ones to my students and teachers, in the final moments of my last class at UCSB, the one I called Hope That Works, and this is the last of my testimonies here on the subject:

Courage comes from a core of love. In love with Earth, even beyond hope, we can keep on coming on, courageously until the end of our days.

Earth Is Our Next Home

14

Years back, I went on a vision quest near Point Conception, California, the holy Western Gate of the Chumash people from this part of the Earth. I had a very simple shelter, an open shell constructed of a piece of canvas stretched over a bower of bent branches secured by strong twine. It was long enough to lie down in, but not tall enough to stand up under. I had to sit or lie down and stretch my legs as best I could, as I'd been instructed not to walk around, but to stay in place and focus on my task.

Archie Fire Lame Deer of the Santa Barbara Indian Center was conducting the ceremony for me, and his instructions were, "See what you can see," before he left me on my own and went to tend to the fire that he lit for me in the frosty morning of the first day.

For three days and nights I stayed rooted to the spot, with a half-gallon of water, no food, and a thin blanket. I wish I'd brought a warmer blanket, because it was very cold at night and I found it impossible to sleep soundly.

I persevered through the cold nights and the sweaty hot days. But I found a way to endure. It was as if my body had its own knowledge of what to do. The mental part of me also acted, and my spirit was illuminated, both day and night. My spirit was a bright light in those astoundingly dark nights, far from the city of Santa Barbara.

Looking back now, I think if I had been an outside observer looking down on myself, I might have seen a glow, maybe even a point of light from time to time, as if one of those grains of light I observed in the dark sky had fallen to Earth and had arisen in a being born of Earth.

It's good to have experiences like this to remind us of who we are. I saw that I was a simple yet immensely powerful being that had arisen in presence within a sacred web of life. I saw myself cycling through light

Marc McGinnes, 2018. *Photo by Isaac Hernández.*

and darkness. I saw divinity everywhere I looked; everything I looked at showed me the divinity in me.

In my divinity and imperfection, I saw myself called into being and nurtured to my purpose. I saw the circularity of time and space, and even the unity of space time. I stared into eternity. I saw myself die and yet continue to be and to take up other forms.

Today I see that my life is coming to its final opportunities to come to wisdom about who I am, where I am, why I am and what it is I am to do.

Here and now, I'm blessed to be mostly at peace. This is grounded in my love for the whole Earth and my courage to continue to be a voice for its well-being. It's a kind of active peace that is far, far, far from tired resignation.

Right now is the time to work harder than ever to make Earth our next home.

The Earthangels Are Coming

Epilogue

Recently, I attended a presentation at UCSB to hear Dr. Sarah Jaquette Ray, a professor of environmental studies at Humboldt State University, speak to her topic: "Coming of Age at the End of the World, Eco Grief and the Climate Generation."

I was moved deeply by what she had to say. When I walked out of the room, filled with mostly youthful students, I felt the urge to go outdoors.

I wandered out onto the balcony and surveyed the view from four stories up. I took it all in—the horizon, the vast sky, the blue ocean—and within a few moments, I just burst into tears.

Decades ago, when I first set eyes on the glowing photograph *Earthrise*, I felt myself touched in a profoundly deep place, a place way beyond tactics and strategies. I was in the presence of love. Big love.

As I educated myself with ecological and environmental know-how, I couldn't quite see the overriding premise. But now I can. All these years, I was holding down the fort. Me. An Earthling. Holding down the fort.

I'm an old guy now, who's losing some of his edge. I'm feeling a little dusty and achy. I've been waiting—waiting and holding down the fort. That's a lot of pressure despite all the joys I've gotten over the years.

But standing on the balcony, somehow, I got it. I'm here, just in time, to welcome those to whom the torch is being passed. There are Earthangels already here, and I was just in the presence of some of the newest to arrive!

Now I know. I was holding down the fort for them. The light I have borne is a light in those who have arrived and are arriving to do their part in the years to come.

Just in time.

Thanks and Acknowledgments

I sing the Thank You Song of heartfelt gratitude to those many
of my Earthangel friends and colleagues who made this possible.

**For those whose generous financial support
made this book possible,
to you I sing:**

Katy Allen

Susan Bowers

Jean and Peter Schuyler

John and Suzanne Steed

John Woodward

Seyburn Zorthian

**For those members of the team of coaches
and editors who made this book possible,
to you I sing:**

Nancy Black

Owen Duncan

Isaac Hernández

Quike Hernández

Katey O'Neill

Ilene Segalove

**For those whose research work
and other assistance made this book possible,
to you I sing:**

Savannah Bertrand

Lauren Lankenau

Zak Liebhaber

Clementine Powell

Rosina Saeed

Cynthia Torres

**For those friends and colleagues from the three organizations with whom I have worked most closely for the past many years and whose ongoing and effective work has kept my spirits up and made this book possible,
to you I sing:**

The Community Environmental Council (see photo below)

The Environmental Defense Center (see photo below)

The UCSB Environmental Studies Program (see photo below)

**For those friends and colleagues from the many other nonprofit organizations in Santa Barbara whose ongoing and effective work in the community inspire me greatly and who have made this book possible,
I sing to you:**

Art From Scrap

Bioneers Channel Islands Restoration

California Regional Environmental Education Community Network Central Coast

Citizens Planning Association and Foundation

Conception Coast Project

ECOFaith of Santa Barbara

Explore Ecology

Friends of Montecito Hot Springs

Gaviota Coast Conservancy

Get Oil Out!

Goleta Valley Beautiful

Gray Whales Count

Green Business Santa Barbara County

Heal the Ocean

Land Trust for Santa Barbara County

Los Padres Forest Watch

More Mesa Preservation Coalition (MMPC) .

NatureTrack

Nuclear Age Peace Foundation

Ocean Futures

Ojai Raptor Center

Pesticide Awareness and Alternatives Coalition

Project Clean Water

San Marcos Foothills Coalition

Santa Barbara Audubon Society

Santa Barbara Beekeepers Association

Santa Barbara Bicycle Coalition

Santa Barbara Botanic Garden

Santa Barbara Bucket Brigade

Santa Barbara Car Free

Santa Barbara Channelkeeper

Santa Barbara County Action Network

Santa Barbara Hikes!

Santa Barbara Maritime Museum

Santa Barbara Museum of Natural History

Santa Barbara Permaculture Network

Santa Barbara Urban Creeks Council

Santa Barbara Wildlife Care Network

Santa Barbara Zoo

Santa Cruz Island Foundation

Santa Ynez Chumash Environmental Office

SBCC Center for Sustainability

Sierra Club, Los Padres Chapter

South County Energy Efficiency Partnership

Sprout Up

Sustainability Project of Santa Barbara

The Trust for Public Land

Ty Warner Sea Center

Wilderness Youth Project

For all of the women and men and boys and girls who have been my students and teachers throughout my life—far, far too many to list all of your names here, I sing to you my heartsongs of gratitude, that they may bestow blessings in abundance on each and all of you.

And for Earth, and all of its communities of life, and for all of the future generations of Earthlings who are coming, I sing for you too.

Community Environmental Council staff: Back row: Sigrid Wright, Julia Blanton, Iris Kelly, Allegra Roth, Michael Chiacos, Cameron Gray, Zachary Pettit, April Price. Front row: Lisa Hill, Kathi King, Nicole Wald, Becca Summers, Emily Miller. *Photo by Sarita Relis from the 2018 CEC Green Gala, courtesy of Community Environmental Council.*

Environmental Defense Center staff: (left to right) Linda Krop, Maggie Hall, Alicia Roessler, Kristen Hislop, Kaleena Quarles, Owen Bailey, Tara Messing, Chile McConnell, Brian Trautwein, Betsy Weber (not pictured: Kathy Hunt, Pearl Lee). *Photo courtesy of Environmental Defense Center.*

University of California, Santa Barbara Environmental Studies department faculty and staff: Back Row (left to right): Erinn O'Shea, Summer Gray, Andrea Adams, Jordan Clark, Celia Alario, Alex Garcia, Jennifer Martin, Michael Brown, David Pellow, Pete Alagona, Robert Heilmayr, Hannah Bone, Cheryl Hutton, and Claudia Tyler. Middle Row (left to right): Lisa August-Schmidt, Mel Manalis, Ed Keller, Jake Fernandes, Carla D'Antonio, Greg Graves, Quentin Gee, Martin Rodriguez, Thea Cremers, Matto Mildenberger, Eric R.A.N. Smith, Simone Pulver, and Ian Castillo. Front Row (left to right, kneeling): David Stone and Eric Zimmerman. *Photo courtesy of Eric Zimmerman, UCSB ES Department.*

Marc, Fern, Drue.

Lightning Source UK Ltd.
Milton Keynes UK
UKHW040832150819
348014UK00001B/7/P